BOBBINS

Bobbins are usually used in sets of 4. This book looks at braids using up to 16 bobbins.

They are made of smooth wood, and lead-filled to provide extra weight. This weight varies, lighter ones being used for finer braids, and heavier ones for thicker braid. Weights of 100 or 70 grammes are common although 37 and 240 grammes are also available.

The most important factor is that each bobbin is equally weighted. If this point is overlooked, uneven braiding can occur.

COTTON LEADERS

Each bobbin is wound with a cotton leader. This is a thread of crochet cotton or similar, cut to a length of approximately 120cm for each bobbin. The two ends of the threads are knotted together with an overhand knot and attached to the bobbin using a lark's head knot. The purpose of the leader is to prevent wastage of precious warp threads by allowing the bobbins to hang at the correct height whilst the end of the warp is braided.

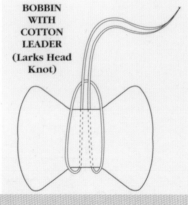

BOBBIN WITH COTTON LEADER (Larks Head Knot)

WEIGHT BAG

This is used to counterbalance the weight of the bobbins and to provide the tension. The bag can be of any construction bearing in mind the weight it must carry. The drawstring is used to attach the bag to the braid being worked. The string must be soft enough to avoid damaging the braid, yet have enough grip to prevent it from slipping. Ideally a fine Kumihimo braid should be used.

A method for making a weight bag:

1) Cut fabric 30 x 12cm, sew 2 hems, allowing room for the drawstring.

2) Fold in half and sew 2 side seams, making sure not to sew over the drawstring hem.

3) Turn inside out and thread the drawstring along both hems. Join the ends of the drawstring with an overhand knot.

The weights used inside the bag can be of any form. Fishing, or scale weights are an easily obtainable option. The amount of weight required is roughly half that of the total bobbins used.
More details on Page 11.

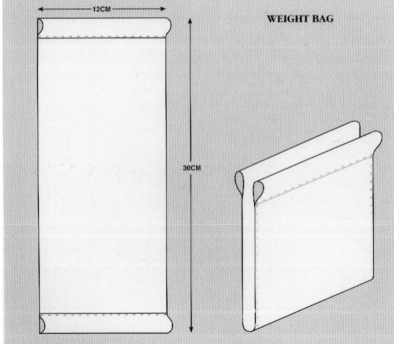

12CM

30CM

WEIGHT BAG

CHOPSTICK

This, or a knitting needle substitute, is used to secure the braid whilst work is not in progress *(See page 9 & 12)*.

The chopstick must be smooth to avoid snagging the threads. If the chopstick has a fine point, this can be used to loosen the threads evenly whilst winding bobbins up or down.

'S' HOOK

These small metal 'S' shaped hooks can be obtained from most hardware shops. An S hook is only used at the start of braiding to attach the weight bag to the warp.

WARPING POSTS

Two smooth posts are needed for winding a warp, the warp being the group of threads to be braided. At least one must be made moveable in order to allow the alteration of distance between them, thus varying the length of warp.

During the winding process the posts must remain stationary. They must have sufficiently weighted bases, or be clamped down in some manner.

THREADS

A smooth lustrous silk is the traditional medium for Kumihimo. This illustrates the structure of the braid with the play of light and shade, and gives a precise finish to the stitches made.

However, the choice of thread is limitless. Varieties and mixtures of texture, thickness and colour can be used, as well as more unusual items such as leather, fabric, wire or paper. the choice of thread will obviously affect the appearance of the final braid and should therefore be selected for the appropriate project.

Also needed will be a supply of crochet cotton or similar. This will be used to tie off the threads and the finished braids.

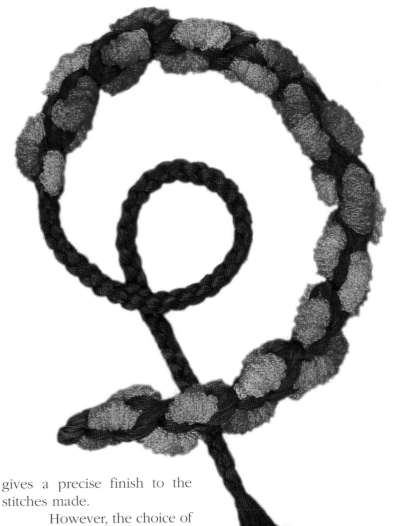

Photograph 3:
Braid using unusual threads (See Page 98)

CHOICE OF WARP THREADS

Before any winding can commence various decisions about the warp must be reached. Each decision will affect the braid to be produced.

1. Type of thread.
2. Number and ratio of colours.
3. Number of threads per bobbin.
4. Length of threads to be wound.

1. THREAD TYPE

As we have seen, the choice of thread is endless. It is also possible to use a combination of different materials in one braid. This can be done either by winding the different material onto separate bobbins, or by mixing the various threads on a single bobbin. This also applies to the mixing of colours.

2. COLOURS

This is an important decision as it can dramatically change the appearance of the braid. The braid sequence produces the structure, or shape, of the braid, but it is the colours that give the pattern on that structure. Therefore the number of different colours used to make the warp, and their proportions will determine the pattern created whilst braiding. As the pattern on a braid structure can be altered by rearranging the initial colour layout, several patterns can be achieved using the same warp.

It is a constant source of amazement that striking changes can take place simply by rearranging this colour layout *(refer to Page 16 for more working details)*. Any colour combination can be used, but it is worth remembering that the stronger the contrast in colour, the more defined the pattern.

3. NUMBER OF THREADS

The number of threads wound on each bobbin, and the total number of bobbins used, dictates the thickness of the final braid. It is worth noting that the finer braids require more stitches per centimetre and therefore take longer to produce. The quantity of thread wound on each bobbin does not have to be uniform and can be used to create unusual effects *(see photograph 4, below)*.

4. LENGTH

As it is difficult to do a satisfactory join of threads whilst braiding,, it is necessary to know the 'take up' of threads in order to wind the correct length, this take up will vary depending on the following:

* *Type of thread*
* *Braid sequence*
* *Weight of bag tension*
* *Personal tension*

In some braiding sequences it will also vary from bobbin to bobbin. Experience soon shows that sampling is the only accurate way to calculate the take up of a final piece. However, as a rough guide the following can be used; if a 1 metre warp length is wound it will produce approximately 60 centimetres of braid.

Photograph 4: Distorted Braids (See Page 98)

WINDING THE WARP

METHOD 1:
INDIVIDUAL BOBBINS

This is not a Japanese method but an easier, more adaptable one to learn. It is advisable to wind even numbers of threads onto the bobbins, as this avoids having to tie in the odd one.

Place the warping posts apart at your required warp length. Secure the thread at post A and wind clockwise around the posts. Keep the threads parallel. Winding from A to B creates one thread for the bobbin. Winding back from B to A creates a second thread. Continue winding until sufficient number of threads have been wound for one bobbin. Keeping the threads hanging from post B, lift the thread off the start/finish post (A) and attach this end to the bobbin as shown on the next page.

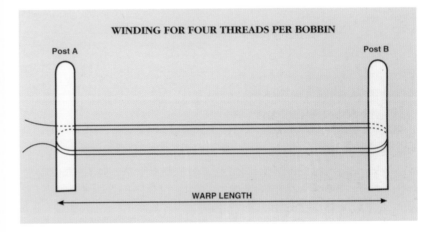

WINDING FOR FOUR THREADS PER BOBBIN

Post A

Post B

WARP LENGTH

BEGINNERS EXAMPLE

All the previous information can be rather confusing to the beginner; but will become clearer with experience. For this reason the four decisions for an example warp to make braid 4A (see page 33), a 4 bobbin braid, have been listed:

<u>1</u>
Thread type: 2 ply wool

<u>2</u>
Number and ratio of colours: two contrasting colours in equal proportions. Two of the bobbins wound with one colour, the two remaining bobbins wound with the other.

<u>3</u>
Number of threads per bobbin: Four.

<u>4</u>
Thread length: 1 metre.

These decisions can now be used in the following winding procedure. Guidelines are given in coloured boxes at the end of each section

BEGINNERS EXAMPLE

*Set winding posts 1 metre apart. Wind 4 threads of the first colour.
(A to B to A twice).
Attach the bobbin as shown on next page and repeat this once more for another bobbin. Now use your second colour and wind 4 threads on to each of the two remaining bobbins.*

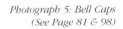

*Photograph 5: Bell Caps
(See Page 81 & 98)*

KNOT FOR ATTACHING WARP THREADS TO COTTON LEADER

1. Hold the leader between your left thumb and index finger. Take the warp threads under the leader and hold between thumb and index finger.

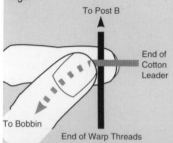

2. Take the end of the warp threads over the thumb to the left, behind the warp threads and down over the leader. Hold in place with thumb and finger.

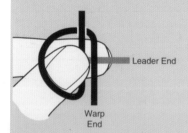

3. Make a small loop with the end of the leader.

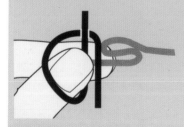

This replaces the thumb when the warp is pushed off the thumb and onto the loop. Pull tight on the warp end until the knot 'clicks' into place.

The knot can easily be released by pulling the end of the cotton leader.

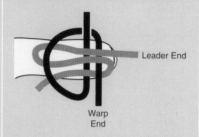

An alternative knot such as overhand or reef knot can be used if this one proves too difficult for the beginner.

When the threads are attached, carefully wind them on to the bobbin until approximately 40 centimetres from post B. Secure the bobbin with a slip knot as shown.

SLIP KNOT

1. Hold the bobbin in the left hand so that the thread comes from underneath and away from you.

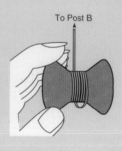

IT IS IMPORTANT TO HOLD THE BOBBIN LIKE THIS AT ALL STAGES.

2. Using the right hand, form a loop making sure the threads cross over as shown in diagram.

3. Place the slip knot on to the bobbin, by passing the bobbin into the loop from underneath.

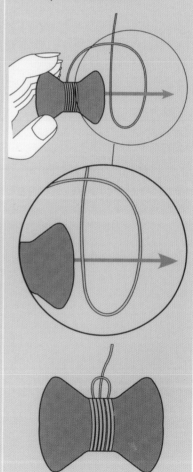

The bobbin should now hang from the post (B) by loops in the threads. Either leave the bobbin in this position, or remove to hang on another suitable point (coat hook or door knob will do). Repeat this process using the appropriate thread for each bobbin until all bobbins are wound and hanging together.

Take a piece of crochet cotton through all the loops on all of the bobbins. Knot the cotton, thus securing all the threads together. Then knot the cotton again to form a loop. This will be used when attaching the chopstick.

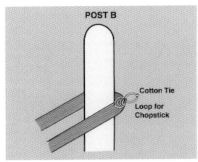

POST B

Cotton Tie

Loop for Chopstick

Lift the warp off its post and bring to the Marudai. Push the cotton loop down through the central hole and secure by slipping the chopstick through the loop from below the Marudai.

BEGINNERS EXAMPLE

Secure the warp on the Marudai as directed. Now proceed to 'Arranging the Bobbins' on page 11.

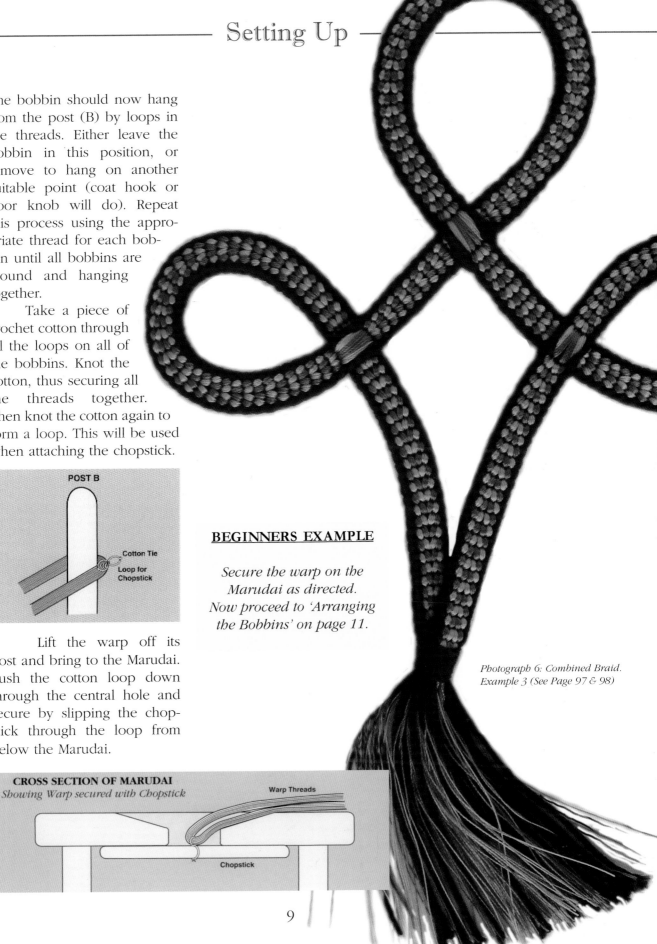

Photograph 6: Combined Braid. Example 3 (See Page 97 & 98)

CROSS SECTION OF MARUDAI
Showing Warp secured with Chopstick

Warp Threads

Chopstick

9

METHOD 2:
SECTIONAL WARP

This is more suitable for winding longer lengths as the posts are closer together. Odd numbers of threads are also easier to deal with. Place the warp posts half the warp length apart. Secure the end of the thread at post A and wind clockwise. Winding from A to B to A creates just one thread. Wind the required times for one bobbin and secure. Then using crochet cotton, tie a Larks head (see page 4) on one side of the warp approximately 20 centimetres from post A. This is the thread for one bobbin. Do not remove these threads, but repeat the process until the thread for all the bobbins is on the warping posts. Make sure to tie off each group of threads for each bobbin. When this is completed, very tightly tie all the threads together in 2 places (C & D) at a distance of approximately 5 and 6 centimetres from post A. The distance between post A and tie D will dictate the lengths of the tassel. Cut all the threads along post A.

Pass the chopstick through the threads between ties C and D. Now insert the chopstick through the centre of the Marudai. The chopstick needs to be held secure against the underside of the mirror until at least one bobbin has been attached. This can be achieved by placing the weight bag on top of the warp resting on the mirror (diagram 2).

Separate the thread for one bobbin (marked by a cotton tie). Attach the bobbin and wind as shown in method one. Repeat the process until all bobbins are wound.

Preparation can be approached in other ways including the use of pre-cut warps. Whichever method is used, care should be taken in getting the threads to lie straight and even. Failure to do so can result in a poor quality braid.

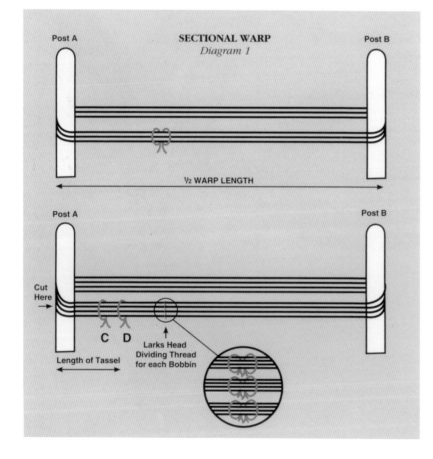

SECTIONAL WARP
Diagram 1

Post A   Post B

½ WARP LENGTH

Post A   Post B

Cut Here →

C   D

Length of Tassel

Larks Head
Dividing Thread
for each Bobbin

ARRANGING THE BOBBINS

Arrange the bobbins around the Marudai so that the starting position and initial colour lay-out is correct for the chosen braid. The bobbins should hang evenly, approximately half-way down the legs. Loosen the slip knot and wind or unwind gently to alter the height of the bobbins. Alternatively, remove the slip knot and retie in a new position.

WEIGHTING

Fill the weight bag with appropriate weights. This will vary depending on the braid-maker, threads used, bobbins and desired braid. Weighting is often overlooked as a variable. It can be particularly important to get right in braids that use bobbins wound with different threads or ones containing unusual threads. Experimenting is the best way to understand what weight will work best under different circumstances.

As a rough guide add up the total weight of bobbins and use about half that in the weight bag.

Remember: The more weight, the more elongated the stitches, and slacker and softer the braid. The less weight, the more compact the stitches and tighter the braid.

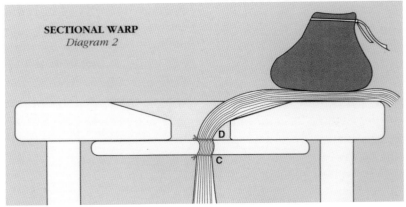

SECTIONAL WARP
Diagram 2

BEGINNERS EXAMPLE

Arrange the threads across the mirror by moving the bobbin positions, so that one colour lies North and South and the other lies East and West.

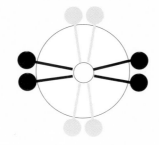

Attach one end of the 'S' hook onto the drawstring of the weight bag. Attach the other end onto the loop through which the chopstick is resting. Now that the weight bag is creating a counterbalance to the bobbins, the chopstick can be removed and braiding commenced.

Photograph 7: Difference in Weight Bag tension. More weight was used when making the left-hand braid, whilst less weight was used for the right-hand one. (braid details on Page 98).

11

Working

Kneeling is the traditional working position for making Kumihimo. This is an everyday and comfortable position for the Japanese, but not necessarily for the English. It is important to be comfortable whilst working so that you can concentrate on your braiding. If this means sitting, or standing to work, make sure to raise the Marudai to a comfortable height. Alternatively a small foot stool could be used. This should raise you just enough to take the pressure off the ankles and enable the kneeling position to be achieved.

Braiding is carried out by the simultaneous movement of two bobbins to a new position. The movements are made by lifting the threads rather than the bobbins. Lift from a point above the bobbin but below the mirror. Do not pinch the threads but allow them to run freely over your fingers so that the tension from the bobbins remains uniform under movement.

BEGINNERS EXAMPLE

Do not start working at this stage.
Read this chapter now and refer back to it after Chapter 4.

Generally the threads at the front, closest to you, and to the right are lifted on the four fingers. Threads at the back, or left, are lifted using the thumbs. These hand positions are interchanged as they cross the Marudai (see photograph opposite). Work through the chosen sequence of movements smoothly and evenly, adjusting bobbin positions either during or at the end of the sequence to keep the layout precise.

The more precise the angle of movement around the Marudai, the neater the braid!

It is worth noting that when working with several threads on each bobbin, the appearance and structure of the braid is altered depending on whether the threads lie flat or are twisted across the mirror. Threads should remain either flat or uniformally twisted whilst working.

Fluctuation in this factor can result in uneven braiding.

Keep repeating the sequences until you are familiar with the movements, then concentrate on the centre of your work, known as the 'Point of Braiding'. This is the shape created by the intersection of threads at the centre of the Marudai. It is a vital reference point and familiarity of this 'Point of Braiding' will enable the braider to see which is the next move in the sequence and if errors have been made. It is the position of the threads that is the true guide, not the position of the colours as these are not necessarily constant. However, do be aware of the colour positions as they often provide an early warning to mistakes being made (note that some patterns may take several sequences before returning to the original colour layout).

As work progresses the weight bag is continually gets lower and the bobbins higher, so frequent re-adjustment must be made to keep the braid even. To do this, insert the chopstick by sliding it under the 'Mirror', and across the threads above the 'Point of Braiding'. This secures the braid preventing the bobbins slipping off centre and falling to the floor. Remove the weight bag and 'S' hook. Re-attach the drawstring of bag directly onto the braid using a larks head knot (see page 4).

Photograph 8: Hands lifting threads with thumbs and four fingers

Further adjustment is carried out by regular movement of the knot up the braid. Do not allow the weight bag to reach the base of the Marudai as this results in a loss of tension. To lower the bobbins, either loosen the slip knot and gently lower, or remove the knot completely before unwinding and retie. Whenever braiding ceases, secure the Marudai by inserting the chopstick. If it is to be left for any length of time, the weight bag should also be removed. This avoids altering the tension of the thread. Remember to check your reference point on the Marudai so that braiding can be resumed from the same working position.

BRAIDING ERRORS

The following illustrates some mistakes you could expect to make whilst braiding and the appropriate remedies.

MIS-MOVE

This is the most common mistake caused by picking up the wrong bobbin, or placing it down in the wrong position. If the mistake is followed by correct braiding, simply reverse the sequence, undoing the braid until the mistake is reached. Now the correct 'Point of Braiding' must be returned by undoing the error.

Work slowly lifting one bobbin at a time taking the highest threads first. This may take some time getting used to but practice makes perfect! When the threads are back in the correct position, work a sequence or two and check that all errors have been removed.

Prevention is, of course, the best cure, so take care and work slowly making sure the bobbins are kept in neat groups avoiding confusion as to which is which.

GETTING LOST

Distraction has left you uncertain as to which move in the sequence you are at. Look at the 'Point of Braiding' for the highest two threads. These were the last ones moved and can be traced back to their original position. Go back until you arrive at a movement, or 'Point of Braiding' you recognise. This problem will occur less as you become more familiar with the braid and are able to 'Read' the thread positions. In the meantime, be sure to work a sequence to the end before stopping, regardless of other mishaps.

BOBBINS TWISTING TOGETHER

If this occurs, your braiding movements are too harsh, causing the bobbins to swing. At the end of a movement, slip your hand down the thread to steady the bobbin in its new position. Having the bobbins at a uniformed height will also help prevent this problem.

LUMPS AND BUMPS

The difference in strength between the right and left hand is sufficient to alter the evenness of a braid. So any extra tugs, or jarring movement, will disrupt the flow of the pattern. Lumps at the change over form one pattern to another are inevitable, although some have smoother transitions than others.

UNEVEN THREADS

If the threads on a bobbin become uneven in tension the resulting braid will contain small puckers of loose threads. To remedy this, insert the chopstick and undo the offending bobbin. Smooth the thread and retie before continuing work.

MOVEMENT OF THE 'POINT OF BRAIDING'

During most braiding sequences the 'Point of Braiding' should remain central and steady. Any fluctuation is due to uneven braiding movements. However any braid sequence that disrupts the even balance of bobbins around the Marudai will cause the 'Point of Braiding' to move, (e.g. Braid 8D). It is normal in these circumstances and should rectify itself with further movements of the sequence. Adding extra weight in the bag will help steady the braid, but do not forget that it will also alter the tension.

Photograph 9 (right): Shell bag. (see page 98)

14

Patterns

In this chapter the braids are grouped together in styles of moves. There are four basic types of movement:

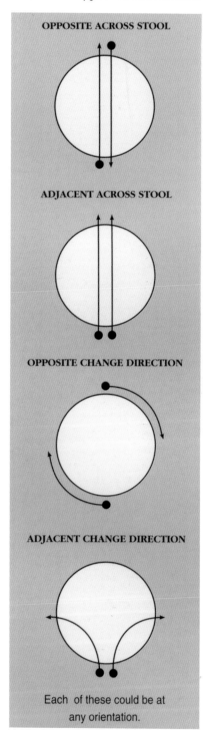

OPPOSITE ACROSS STOOL

ADJACENT ACROSS STOOL

OPPOSITE CHANGE DIRECTION

ADJACENT CHANGE DIRECTION

Each of these could be at any orientation.

The moves work in combinations and variations to create different sequences. These sequences of moves dictate the structure of the braid created. It is advisable to learn the moves with 8 bobbins so that progression to 16 bobbins is better understood.

For every braid structure a multitude of different colour patterns can be created. When bobbins loaded with different coloured threads are used, the path that each colour follows can be altered to create new patterns on a braid structure. This is achieved by rearranging the position of the bobbins before braiding commences. This is referred to as the 'Initial Colour Layout'. Two colour pattern examples for each braid structure are shown on pages 27-32. Their relevant initial colour layouts are given on pages 98 & 99.

Remember: Braid structure created by the sequence of moves. The pattern on the braid is created by the initial colour layout.

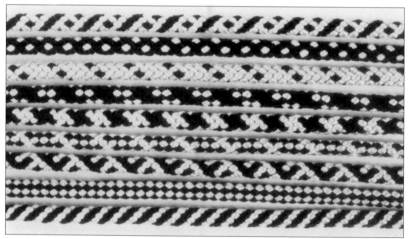

Photograph 10 (top): Pattern changed by different initial colour layouts (details on page 98).
Photograph 11 (below): Braid structure changed by different sequence of moves (details on page 98).

16

DIAGRAMS

Each braiding sequence is explained by following the diagrams. The large circle represents the Marudai surface viewed from above. The small circles represent the position of the bobbins hanging down from the mirror. The arrows show the path the bobbins must take to reach their new positions. The numbers denote the order of movement within the sequence. When the last movement has been reached, return to movement 1. The sequence of moves is repeated until the required braid length is reached. References to 'R/H' and 'L/H' refer to bobbins to be lifted with the right and left hand respectively. 1 & 2 defines the order in which the bobbins must move. This ensures the thread crosses in the correct manner. The point of braiding shown is the position of the threads at the end of the sequence, ready for movement 1.

GRIDS

The following information is not intended for the total beginner as it is an aid for creating new braid patterns not already illustrated.

The drafting grids are a 2-dimensional representation of the braids. The shape of the grids is dependent on the braid structure. The grey lines show the meeting point of two sides, or faces, of braid structure. Each number shows the path and 'Stitches' created by a particular bobbin. The starting positions and designated number of the bobbins is shown on page 26. Remember that the grids are repeatable both top and bottom and that the 2 sides join together when the 3-dimensional braid is formed.

The grids can be used to calculate the colour pattern on a braid prior to production. It has been seen that from the start positions (page 26) each bobbin can be given a number. By relating the to the initial colour layout it is possible to give each number a colour. These colours can then be substituted in place of the numbers on the grid giving the resulting pattern for that particular set up.

BEGINNERS EXAMPLE

Now move on to page 33 to start working braid 4A

Photograph 12:
Combined Braid. Example 2.
(See Page 97 & 98)

INITIAL COLOUR LAYOUT

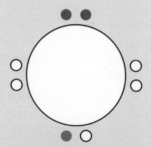

START POSITION NUMBERS

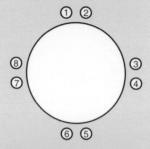

By referring to a chosen initial colour layout with the bobbin starting position numbers as shown, it is possible to give each bobbin number a colour.

This example shows that:
Bobbins 1 & 2 are
Bobbin 6 is
Bobbins 3, 4, 5, 7 & 8 are ◯

The correct grid is now chosen for the braid to be worked, in this case braid 8F.

GRID FOR BRAID 8F

Now the pattern can be revealed by exchanging the numbers with their relevant colour.

Areas containing the number 1 can be replaced with the colour Red.

Areas containing the number 2 can also be coloured Red.

Areas containing the number 6 are coloured Blue.

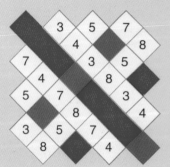

Finally, all the other numbers are coloured White.

This can be repeated several times to give better representation of the finished braid.

The grids can also be worked in reverse. The pattern on a finished braid can be drawn on its relevant grid to reveal the initial colour layout.

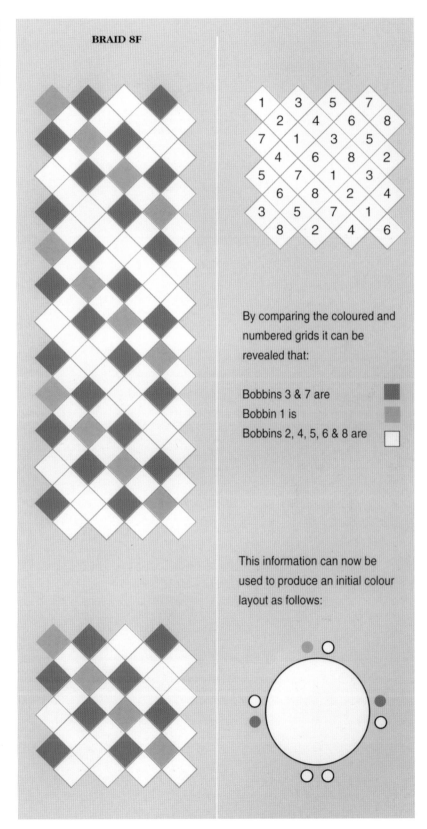

BRAID 8F

By comparing the coloured and numbered grids it can be revealed that:

Bobbins 3 & 7 are
Bobbin 1 is
Bobbins 2, 4, 5, 6 & 8 are

This information can now be used to produce an initial colour layout as follows:

For those who are interested and wish to understand the grids and braid structure better, it is advisable to follow each number through several repeats until the paths that they follow become more obvious. Also, study the paths of the threads as they move around the mirror. This will reveal the 'Sets' of bobbins working together.

GRID FOR BRAID 8H

By following the path created by bobbin 1, it can be noted that the stitches lie in the first and third vertical columns only.

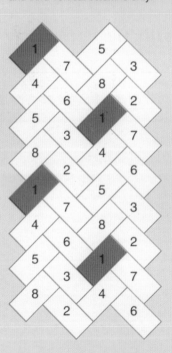

Now follow the path of bobbin 4. These stitches also lie in the first and third columns and always directly under the stitches of bobbin 1.

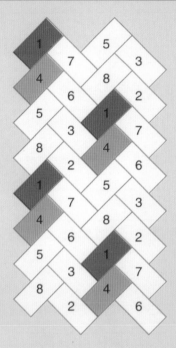

The path of bobbin 5 also lies in these columns, directly under the stitches of bobbin 4.

Bobbin 8 completes these columns, being directly under the stitches of bobbin 5 and above the stitches of bobbin 1.

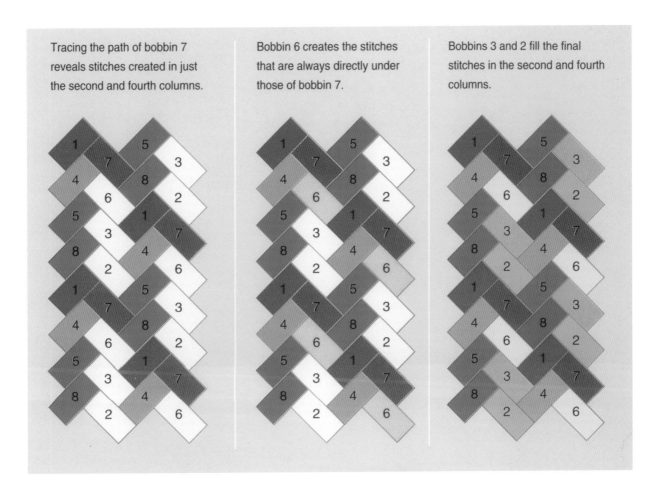

Tracing the path of bobbin 7 reveals stitches created in just the second and fourth columns.

Bobbin 6 creates the stitches that are always directly under those of bobbin 7.

Bobbins 3 and 2 fill the final stitches in the second and fourth columns.

The number patterns revealed show that the first and third columns are built up with the same number order 1, 4, 5 and 8, although the columns are out of step with one another.

The second and fourth columns are similar but with a number order of 7, 6, 3 and 2.

This is reaffirmed by observing the bobbin paths on the mirrors' surface.

Bobbins 1, 4, 5 and 8 all work anti-clockwise whilst remaining in the same order to each other. Bobbins 7, 6, 3 and 2 also remain in order but working in a clockwise direction.

EXPANSION OF BOBBIN NUMBERS

METHOD 1

As a general rule, braids are made with multiples of 4 bobbins. Direct expansion of braids can be achieved by increasing the numbers of bobbins in each 'group' at the start of braiding. The number of moves in the sequence remains the same but the bobbins take longer in returning to their original positions.

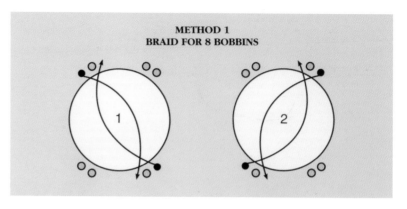

METHOD 1
BRAID FOR 8 BOBBINS

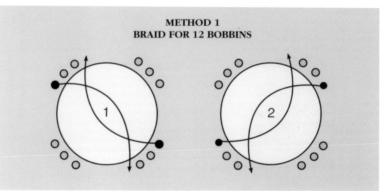

METHOD 1
BRAID FOR 12 BOBBINS

METHOD 2

Alternatively, more groups of bobbins can be added. This will increase the number of moves needed to complete the sequence.

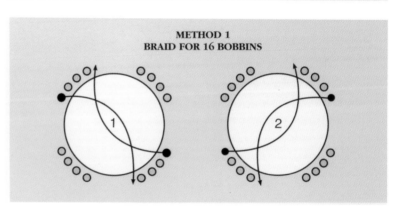

METHOD 1
BRAID FOR 16 BOBBINS

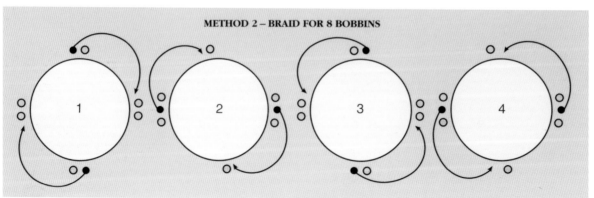

METHOD 2 – BRAID FOR 8 BOBBINS

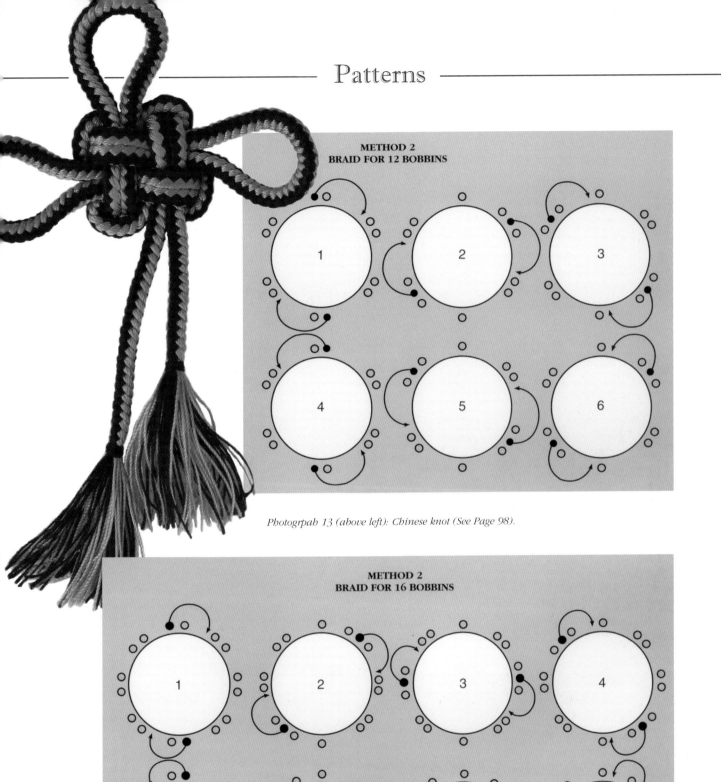

**METHOD 2
BRAID FOR 12 BOBBINS**

Photogrpah 13 (above left): Chinese knot (See Page 98).

**METHOD 2
BRAID FOR 16 BOBBINS**

This information can also be applied to increases beyond 16 bobbins.

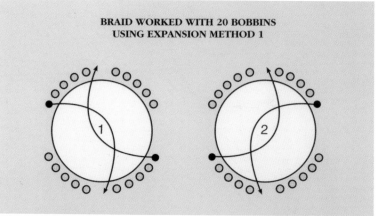

BRAID WORKED WITH 20 BOBBINS USING EXPANSION METHOD 1

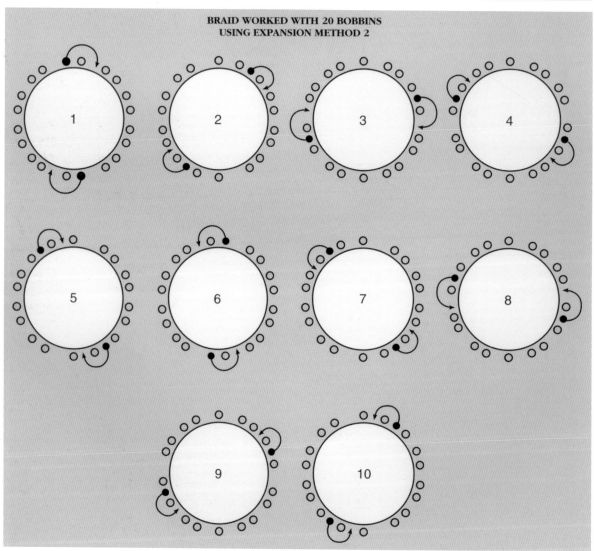

BRAID WORKED WITH 20 BOBBINS USING EXPANSION METHOD 2

Photograph 14 (top right): Camisole top (see page 98)
(bottom right): Paisley shawl (see page 98).

Starting Positions

The following diagrams show the starting positions of bobbins for each braid. Each bobbin is designated a number that can be used in conjunction with the grids. *See page 17.*

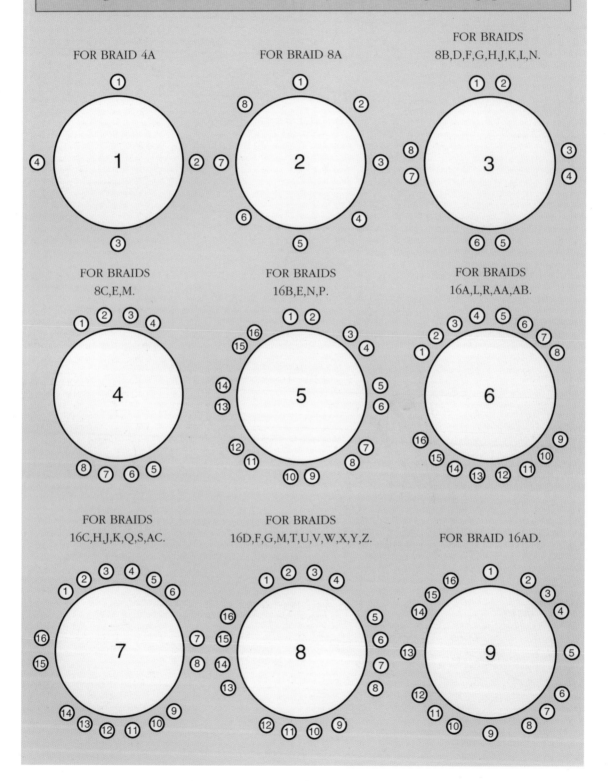

FOR BRAID 4A

FOR BRAID 8A

FOR BRAIDS
8B,D,F,G,H,J,K,L,N.

FOR BRAIDS
8C,E,M.

FOR BRAIDS
16B,E,N,P.

FOR BRAIDS
16A,L,R,AA,AB.

FOR BRAIDS
16C,H,J,K,Q,S,AC.

FOR BRAIDS
16D,F,G,M,T,U,V,W,X,Y,Z.

FOR BRAID 16AD.

4A

4A

8A

8A (Var.)

8B

8B

8C

8C (Var.)

8D

8D

8E

8E

8F

8F

Photograph 15, Colour examples of braids 4A – 8F (top to bottom). (Details on page 98)

Photograph 16, Colour examples of braids 8G – 8N (bottom to top). (Details on page 98)

Photograph 17, Colour examples of braids 16A – 16G (top to bottom). (Details on page 98)

16P (Var.)

16P

16N

16N

16M

16M

16L

16L

16K (Var.)

16K

16J (Var.)

16J

16H

16H

Photograph 18, Colour examples of braids 16H – 16P (bottom to top). (Details on page 99)

Photograph 19, Colour examples of braids 16Q – 16W (bottom to top). (Details on page 99)

16X

16Y

16X

16Y (Var.)

16Z

16Z

16AA

16AA

16AB

16AB

16AC (Var.)

16AC

16AD

16AD

Photograph 20, Colour examples of braids 16X – 16AD (top to bottom). (Details on page 99)

*Cross section
of the braid.*

BEGINNERS EXAMPLE

This is the most basic
Kumihimo braid. However
care is needed to ensure that
the bobbins are crossed in
the correct manner.

For movement 1 the bobbin
threads are lifted with the
right and left hand as
indicated in the diagram. The
hands move simultaneously,
re-positioning the bobbins on
the opposite side of the
mirror. If the movement is
made as a clockwise turn
(Right hand to the right,
left hand to the left); the
threads will cross neatly and
to the correct side of each
other.

For movement 2 the right
arm is crossed under the left
arm as the threads are picked
up. The move is made in an
anti-clockwise direction,
uncrossing the arms to take
the bobbins to their new
positions on the opposite
side of the mirror.
These 2 movements are
continuously repeated to
create a length of braid.

Refer back to chapter 3 for
working hints.
Finishing the braid is
discussed in chapter 5.

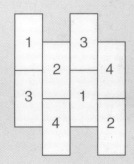

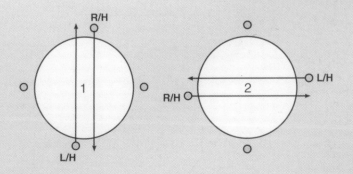

Here two 4A braids (Moves 1 & 2) and (Moves 3 & 4) are worked directly on top of one another to produce an eight bobbin braid that is round and textured.

Variations of this braid can easily be produced by changing the sequence of moves.

The example shown on page 27 is a repeated sequence of moves 1, 2, 1, 2, 3 & 4.

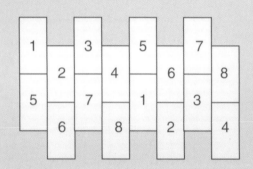

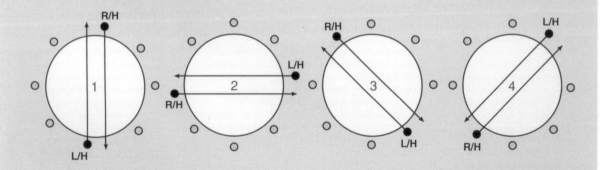

A hard round braid is produced using this sequence.

Here it is important to note that for movement 2, the right arm must be above the left arm as the threads are picked up.

Strip 1	Strip 2	Strip 3	Strip 4	Strip 5	Strip 6
1	3	2	5	7	6
8	1	3	4	5	7
7	6	8	3	2	4
5	7	6	1	3	2
2	4	5	6	8	1
3	2	4	7	6	8
8	1	3	4	5	7
6	8	1	2	4	5
5	7	6	1	3	2
4	5	7	8	1	3
3	2	4	7	6	8
1	3	2	5	7	6
6	8	1	2	4	5
7	6	8	3	2	4
4	5	7	8	1	3
2	4	5	6	8	1

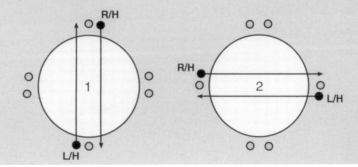

R/H — L/H — 1

R/H — 2 — L/H

8C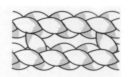

Here two 4A braids (Moves 1 & 2) and (Moves 3 & 4) are worked side by side.

Moves 5 and 6 provide the interlocking stitches to join the two braids together, producing a linked braid.

The size of the links can be varied by altering the number of repeats of each movement.

The example shown on page 27 was made using the following repeated sequence:

Movement 1 & 2 four times.
Movement 3 & 4 four times.
Movement 5 & 6 once.
Movement 1 & 2 twice.
Movement 3 & 4 twice.
Movement 5 & 6 once.

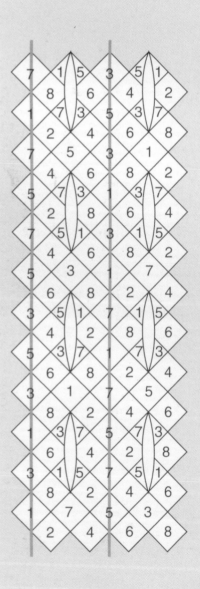

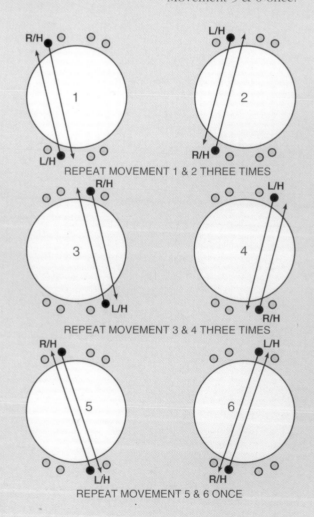

REPEAT MOVEMENT 1 & 2 THREE TIMES

REPEAT MOVEMENT 3 & 4 THREE TIMES

REPEAT MOVEMENT 5 & 6 ONCE

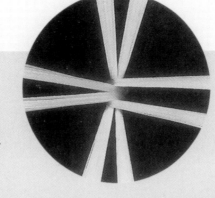

This square braid is an
example of a sequence that
disrupts the balance of the
bobbins around the Marudai.
(Reference:– 'Movement of
the point of Braiding',
Page 14).

Moves 1 and 3 create an
imbalance of weighting but
are immediately countered
by moves 2 and 4.

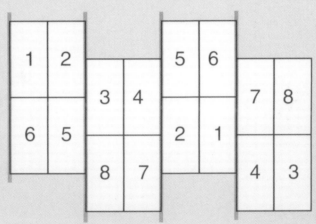

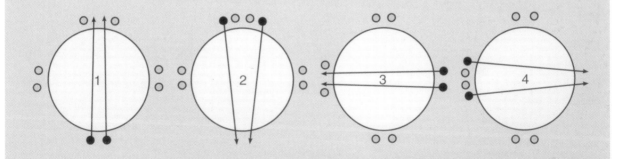

A flat braid with two different sides.

For movement 4, allow the left hand to move slightly before the right hand, to ensure the correct crossover.

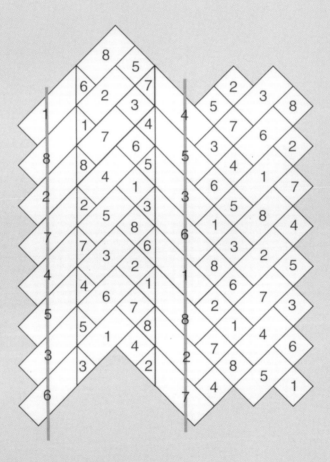

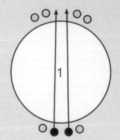

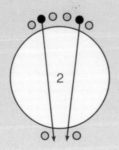

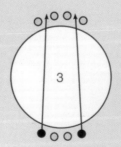

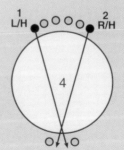

A round hollow braid of plain weave construction. (Under one, over one).

This can be clearly seen by following the paths of the grid.

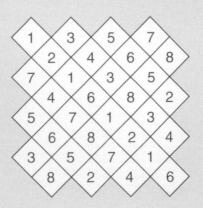

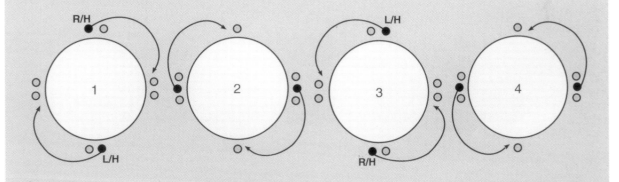

This is identical to the sequence for braid 8F except for the asymetric movement 1.

This opens up the structure to form a plain weave flat braid, each side being the reverse image of the other.

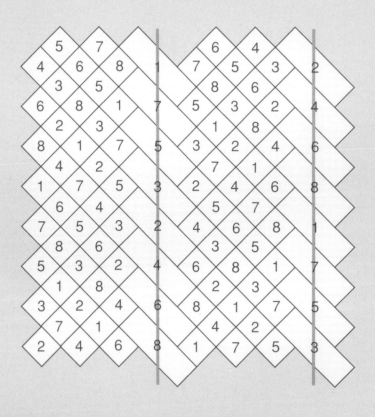

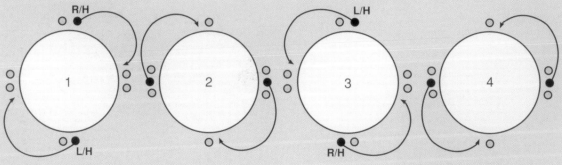

This square braid has
similarities with braid 8F and
produces a Twill weave.
(Under two, over two).

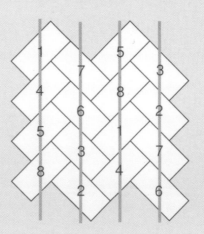

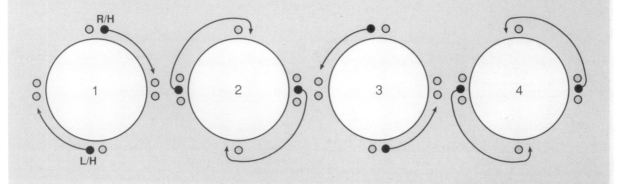

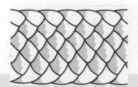

A textured flat braid with well defined edges. Both sides create the same pattern although slightly out of step with one another.

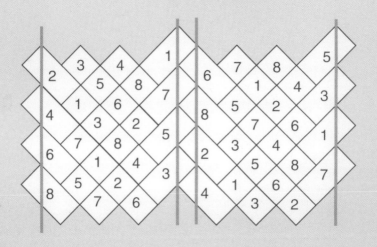

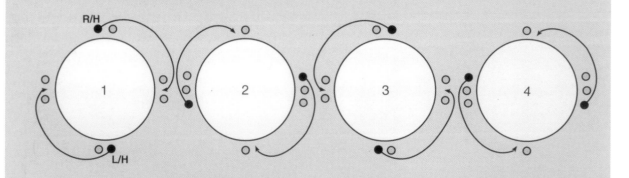

8K

Another flat braid but a smoother, rounder braid than 8J.

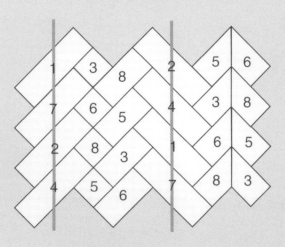

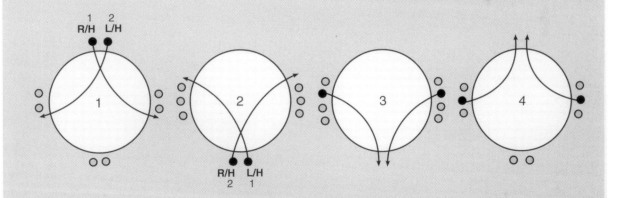

Although the sequence of moves are very similar to that of braid 8K, the resulting braids are quite different.

This flat braid has two contrasting sides; one with large regular stitches, the other being a complex array of many.

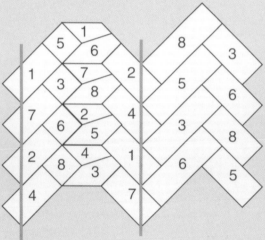

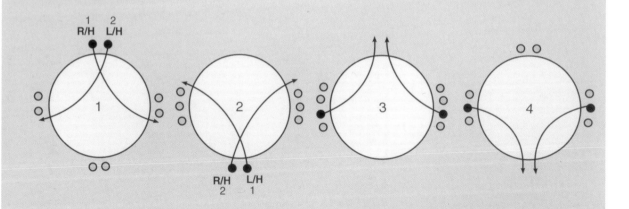

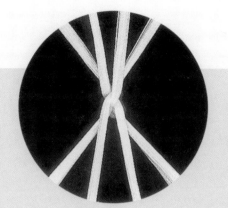

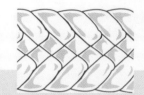

This rectangular braid is comprised of columns of large stitches held secure by tiny central stitches.

It is important to follow the circular motion with the bobbins so that the threads twist correctly at the centre.

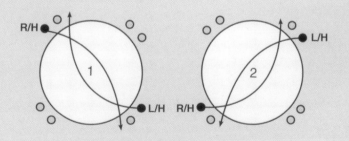

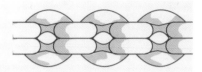

An unusual distorted square braid using a combination of move types; adjacent pairs across the stool and opposite pairs across the stool.

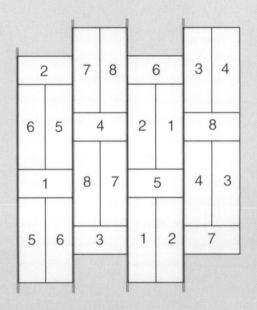

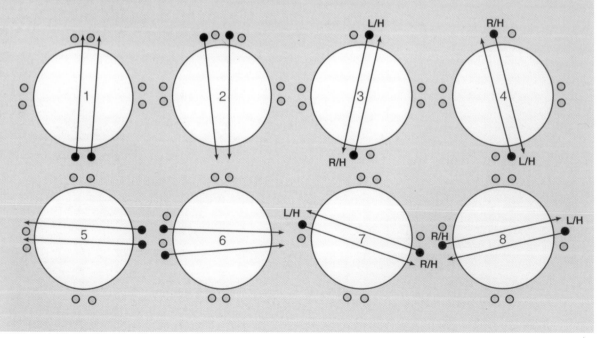

16A ⃝

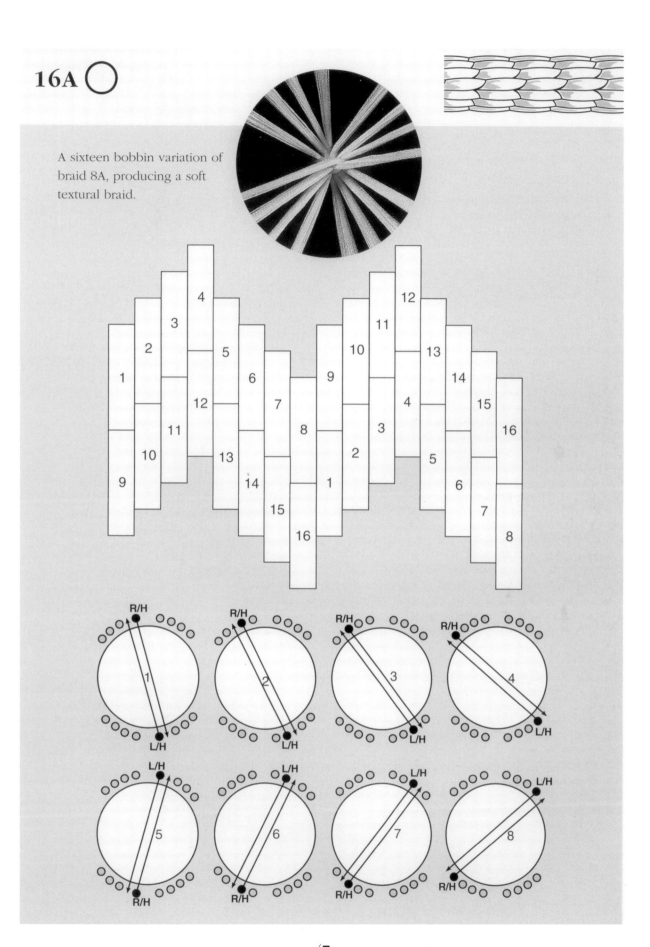

A sixteen bobbin variation of braid 8A, producing a soft textural braid.

47

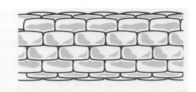

An expansion of braid 8B using extra sets of bobbins and extra moves.

The dense round braid appears to have a pattern that repeats after four sequences. However, with a spiralling repeat within these moves the true structural repeat is after thirty two sequences.

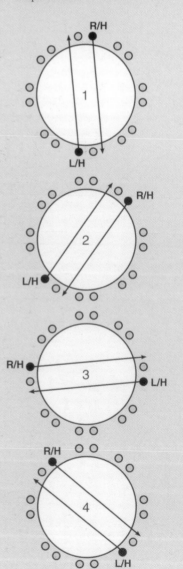

1	3	5	7	2	4	6	8	9
1	3	5	7	2	4	6	8	9
12	14	16	1	3	5	7	2	4
11	13	15	10	12	14	16	1	3
6	8	9	11	13	15	10	12	14
5	7	2	4	6	8	9	11	13
16	1	3	5	7	2	4	6	8
15	10	12	14	16	1	3	5	7
9	11	13	15	10	12	14	16	1
2	4	6	8	9	11	13	15	10
3	5	7	2	4	6	8	9	11
12	14	16	1	3	5	7	2	4
13	15	10	12	14	16	1	3	5
6	8	9	11	13	15	10	12	14
7	2	4	6	8	9	11	13	15
16	1	3	5	7	2	4	6	8
10	12	14	16	1	3	5	7	2
9	11	13	15	10	12	14	16	1
4	6	8	9	11	13	15	10	12
3	5	7	2	4	6	8	9	11
14	16	1	3	5	7	2	4	6
13	15	10	12	14	16	1	3	5
8	9	11	13	15	10	12	14	16
7	2	4	6	8	9	11	13	15
1	3	5	7	2	4	6	8	9
10	12	14	16	1	3	5	7	2
11	13	15	10	12	14	16	1	3
4	6	8	9	11	13	15	10	12
5	7	2	4	6	8	9	11	13
14	16	1	3	5	7	2	4	6
15	10	12	14	16	1	3	5	7
8	9	11	13	15	10	12	14	16
2	4	6	8	9	11	13	15	10

Diagram 1 — R/H, L/H

Diagram 2 — R/H, L/H

Diagram 3 — R/H, L/H

Diagram 4 — R/H, L/H

16C

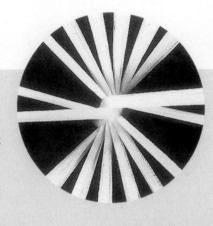

A spiral braid structure consisting of two outer spirals and two inner spirals. Extra tensioning may be required at movement 1 to keep the inner spirals suitably tight. Re-adjusting the bobbins after each sequence can disrupt the flow of this braid making it advisable to let the bobbins remain unadjusted. This will result in the sets of bobbins slowly rotating around the mirror.

At certain points it will become necessary to change the R.H and L.H pick up instructions.

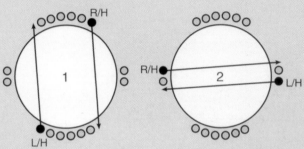

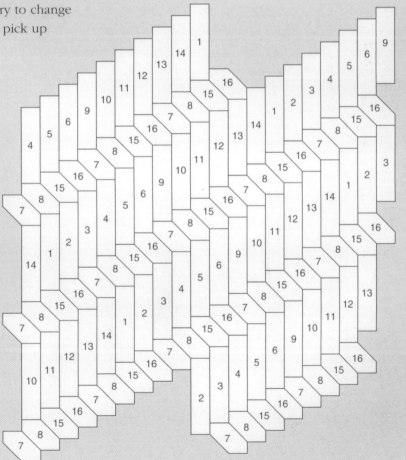

A smooth eight sided braid,
produced using a sixteen
bobbin variation of 8D.

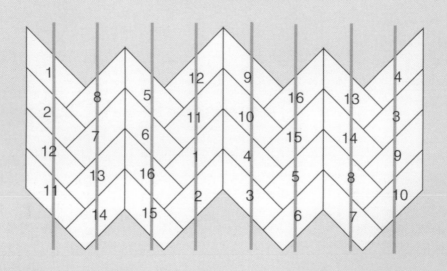

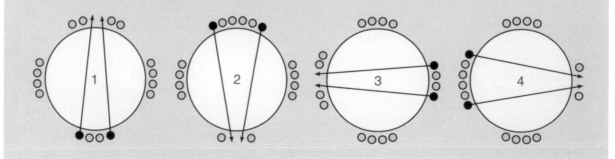

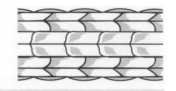

Another sixteen bobbin variation of braid 8D. This time a more knobbly eight sided braid is produced.

An interesting variation of this braid can be made by working repeated sequences of moves: 1, 2, 3, 4. 1, 2, 3, 4.   5, 6, 7, 8. This creates a honeycomb effect. See example on page 29.

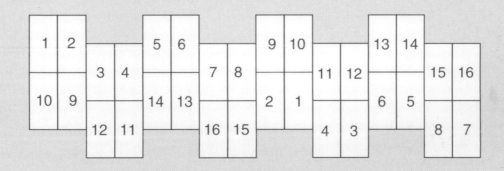

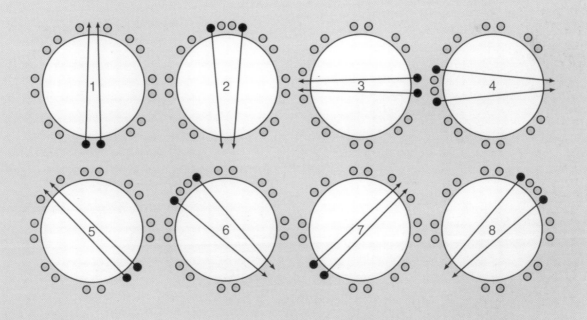

16F ☐

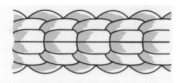

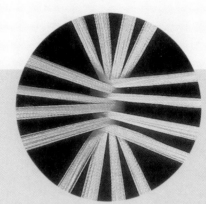

This square braid is yet another variation based on braid 8D.

The solid square structure can be altered by omitting certain moves to create a square braid with indentations. (See page 29) The sequence for this variation is as follows:
1, 2, 3, 4.   5, 6.   1, 2, 5, 6, 7, 8.

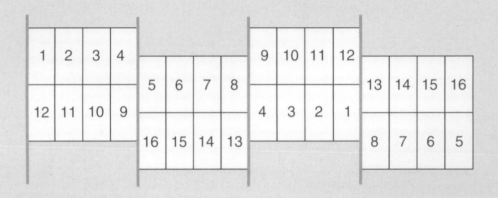

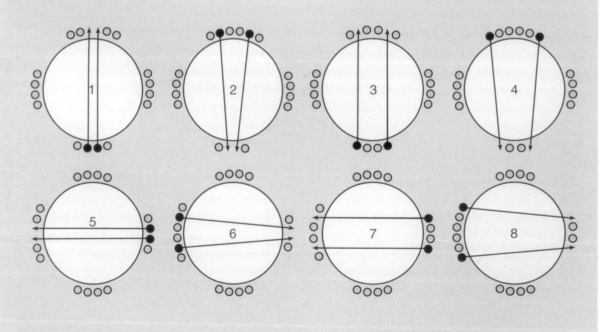

16G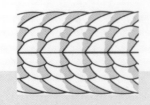

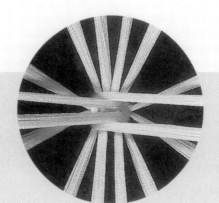

This rectangular braid is produced by using a slight alteration to braid 16F.

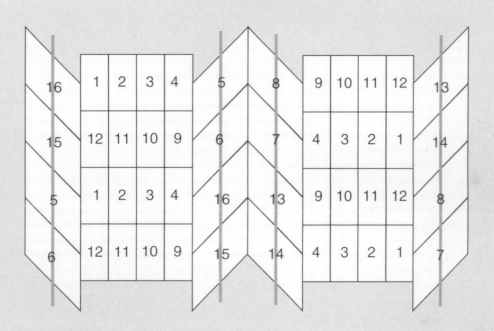

16	1	2	3	4	5		8	9	10	11	12	13
15	12	11	10	9	6		7	4	3	2	1	14
5	1	2	3	4	16		13	9	10	11	12	8
6	12	11	10	9	15		14	4	3	2	1	7

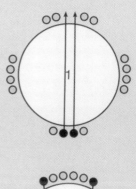
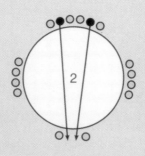
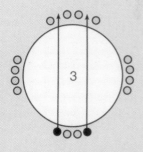

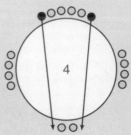
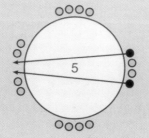
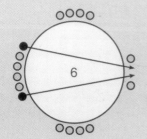

16H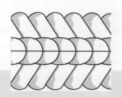

A rectangular braid with long chevron stitches forming the edges.

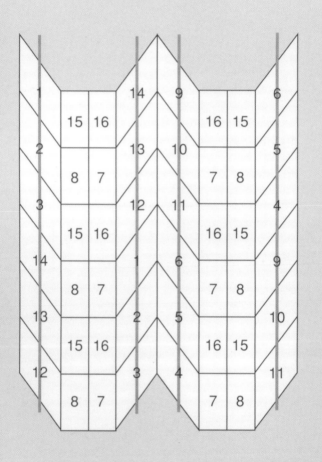

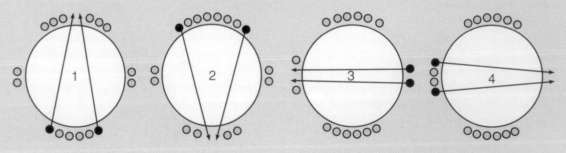

16J

A flatter, wider braid than 16F is created by rearranging the bobbins to increase the sides of the rectangle.

Extra tension may be needed in the East and West pairs of bobbins to prevent gaps appearing in the weave. This should be done by tightening both pairs before making move 7.

By omitting moves similar to the variation of braid 16F, a more sculptured rectangle can be produced.

The sequence of moves is as follows:

1, 2, 3, 4, 5, 6.   7, 8.   1, 2. 7, 8.   1, 2, 3, 4.   7, 8.

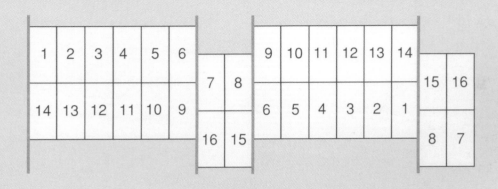

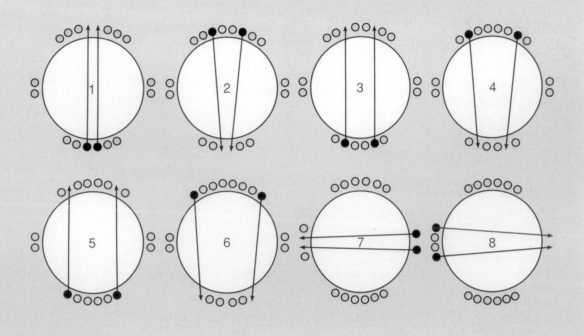

16K

This chainlink braid appears as a complex sequence of moves but it is just the rectangular braid 16J worked at different angles.

The re-adjusting in moves 9 and 18 is achieved by lifting the pairs and sliding them to their new positions ready for move 10 or 1.

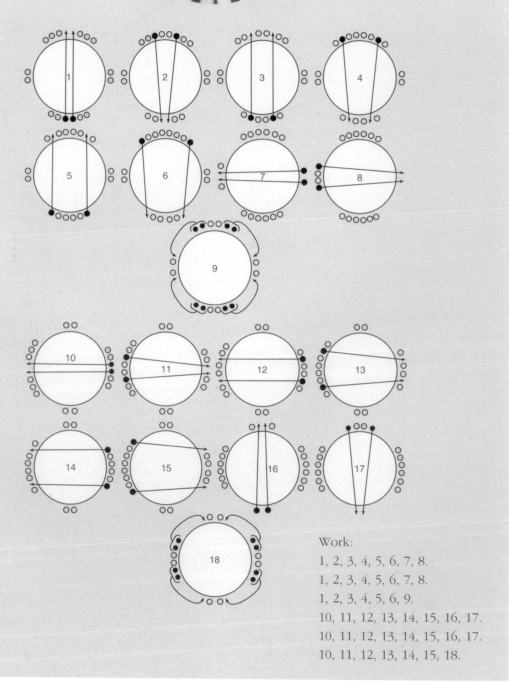

Work:
1, 2, 3, 4, 5, 6, 7, 8.
1, 2, 3, 4, 5, 6, 7, 8.
1, 2, 3, 4, 5, 6, 9.
10, 11, 12, 13, 14, 15, 16, 17.
10, 11, 12, 13, 14, 15, 16, 17.
10, 11, 12, 13, 14, 15, 18.

In order to create the colour pattern variation shown on page 30 it is necessary to do a more complex re-adjustment to keep the colours on the outside of the links.

This is achieved by replacing move 9 with 9A and 9B.

Move 18 is replaced by move 18A and 18B.

Note that in moves 9B and 18B, the three bobbins are lifted as a set over a single bobbin.

The example shown also had the link size increased by adding an extra repeat in each section so that the final sequence ran as follows:

1, 2, 3, 4, 5, 6.	7, 8.
1, 2, 3, 4, 5, 6.	7, 8.
1, 2, 3, 4, 5, 6.	7, 8.
1, 2, 3, 4, 5, 6.	9A, 9B.
10, 11, 12, 13, 14, 15.	16, 17.
10, 11, 12, 13, 14, 15.	16, 17.
10, 11, 12, 13, 14, 15.	16, 17.
10, 11, 12, 13, 14, 15.	18A, 18B.

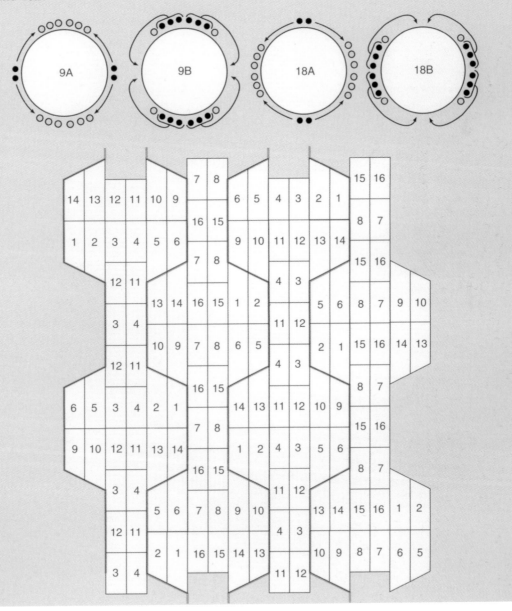

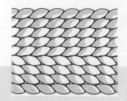

Although both sides of this flat, wide braid appear identical, there are in fact a different number of stitches on each side.

Tension the cross made in move 8 in an East - West direction. This can be reinforced with another gentle pull in movement 2. It will be more effective if the pull is in an East - West direction. The result of all the tensioning is to keep the stitches tight up together, although it can be quite effective to make this braid very loose and soft so that the zig zag of threads can be easily seen.

The grid appears complex but the vertical columns all follow the same number order, though they start at different positions.

1	2	15	6	9	8	10	11	2	16
16	15	3	11	7	9	6	5	15	2
2	3	14	5	10	7	11	12	3	15
15	14	4	12	6	10	5	1	14	3
3	4	13	1	11	6	12	16	4	14
14	13	8	16	5	11	1	2	13	4
4	8	9	2	12	5	16	15	8	13
13	9	7	15	1	12	2	3	9	8
8	7	10	3	16	1	15	14	7	9
9	10	6	14	2	16	3	4	10	7
7	6	11	4	15	2	14	13	6	10
10	11	5	13	3	15	4	8	11	6
6	5	12	8	14	3	13	9	5	11
11	12	1	9	4	14	8	7	12	5
5	1	16	7	13	4	9	10	1	12
12	16	2	10	8	13	7	6	16	1

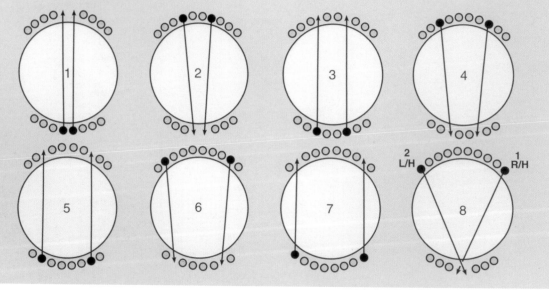

58

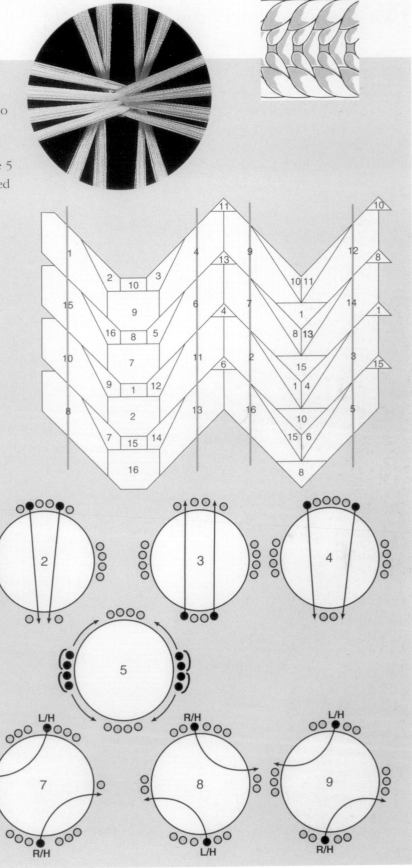

16M ⬡

One face of this braid is smaller than its opposite, so the cross-section is of a truncated triangle.
The re-adjustment in move 5 requires bobbins to be lifted in pairs to their new positions.

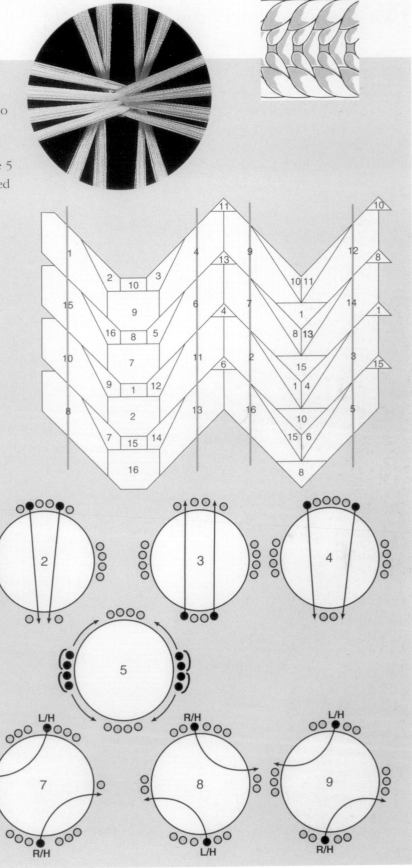

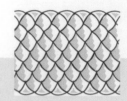

This hollow, round braid is a
sixteen bobbin version of 8F.
The exaggerated hollow
inside the braid is often lost
as the braid is squashed flat.

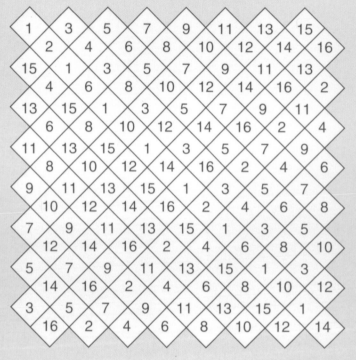

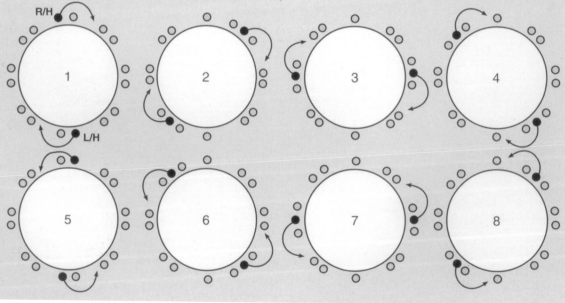

16P

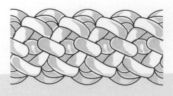

This round honeycomb braid is constructed using two sets of braid 8F worked directly on top of one another. (Moves 1-4 making one set, moves 5-8 creating the other) Here two repeats of each set are made but variations in repeats can alter the density of the honeycomb effect.

The variation of this braid shown on page 30 is similar to braid 16P but the second set (Moves 5-8) work a braid 8D.

This forms straight outer threads compared to the crossed threads of braid 16P. These straight floating threads are exaggerated by working a sequence of the first set (Moves 1-4) repeated three times before a single repeat of the second set. (Moves 5A-8A)

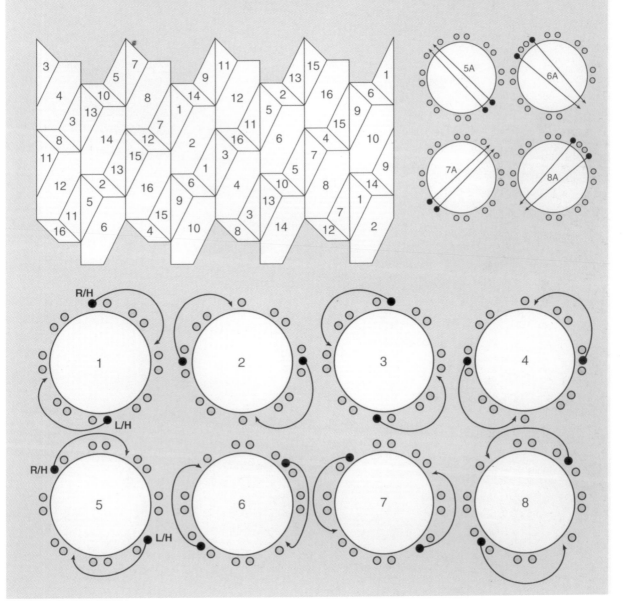

16Q ▭

A flat textured braid also created with moves found in braid 8F and 8D.

Here the arrangement of the sets finds the fine stitches of 8F (Moves 1-4) bordered and positioned by the larger stitches. (Moves 5-8)

The linked version of this braid shown on page 31 follows two repeated sequences of the braid 16Q, but for every third repeat the sequence alters so that moves 5-8 are as follows:

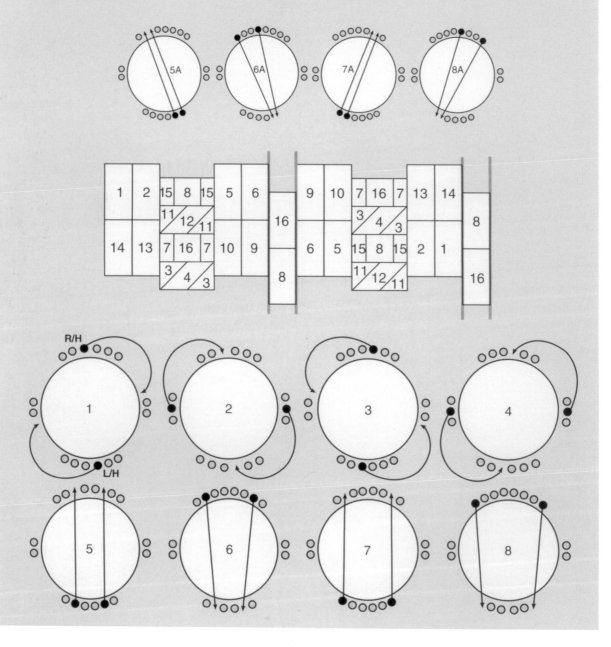

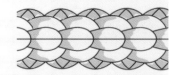

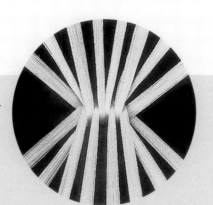

This fancy edged, rectangular braid uses similar moves as in braid 16Q.

The structure of the braid is altered by rearranging the set of bobbins working 8F (Moves 1-4) to border rather than divide the set working in moves 5-8.

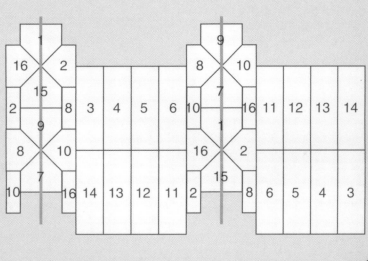

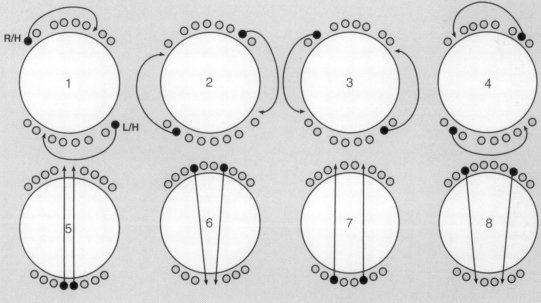

16S

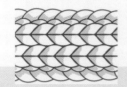

Another arrangement of braids 8F and 8D working in combination.
Here the sequence of the moves creates an oval shaped braid.

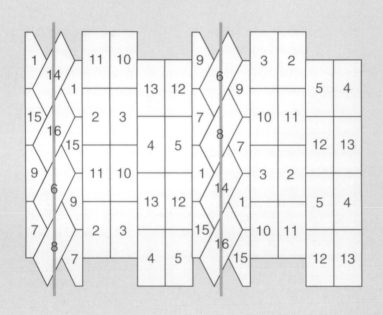

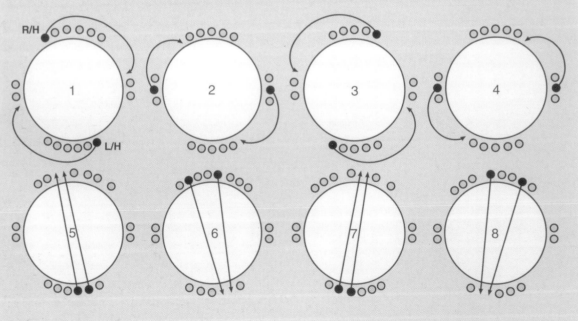

16T

This octagonal braid has movement reminiscent of braid 8F.

The structure however is a direct expansion of the twill weave found in braid 8H.

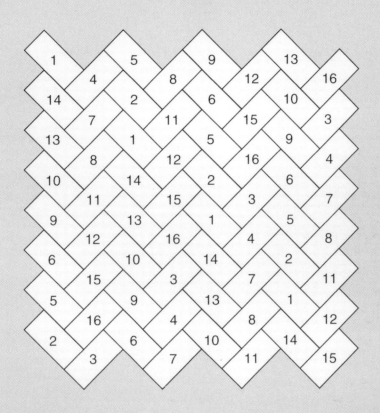

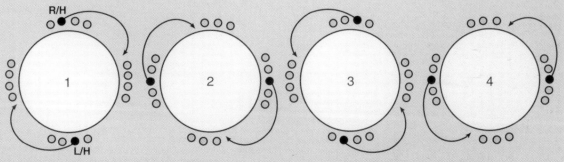

Here a direct expansion of braid 8K is made by increasing the number of bobbins in each group. The resultant braid has one side larger than the other, with a cross section of a truncated triangle.

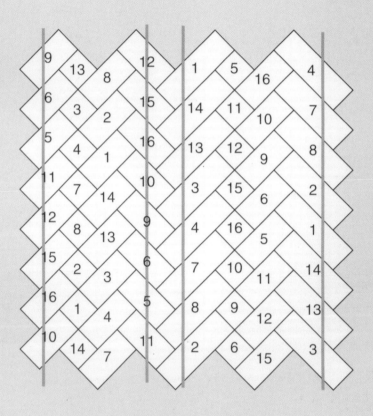

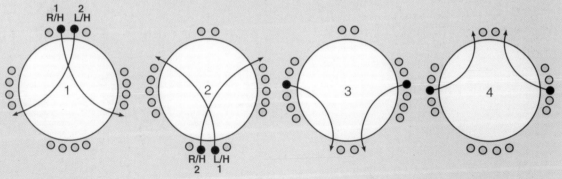

16V

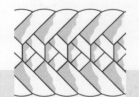

These movements are similar to braid 16U and produce a braid with the same cross section. However the extra moves create some unusually shaped stitches.

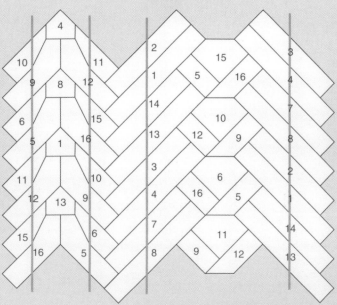

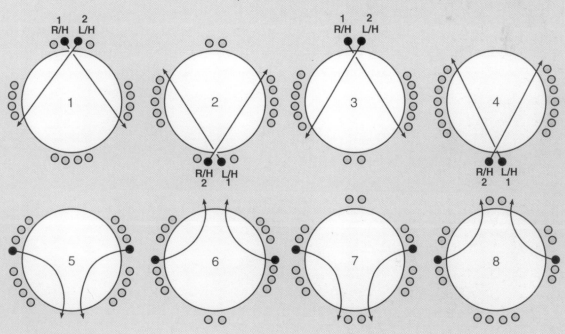

16W

The moves for this braid are similar to braid 16U but the cross section is quite different.

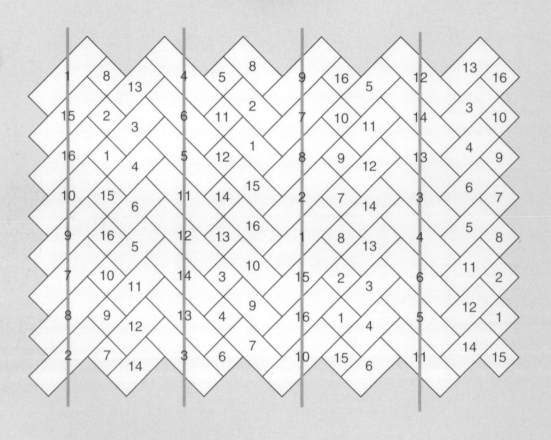

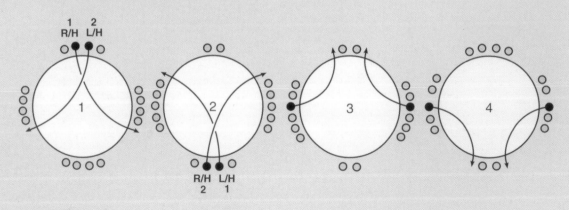

A flat braid with ridged edges, both sides being quite different.

Extra tensioning of the cross created in movement 1 will help keep the braid firm.

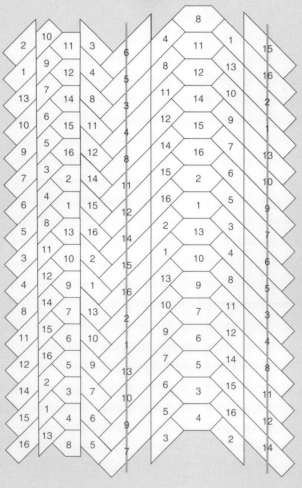

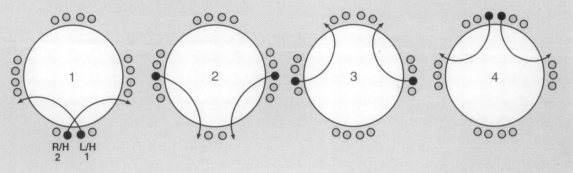

This is a direct expansion of braid 8L. Comparisons can be made with braid 16U.

This is a well defined rectangular braid. Although both sides can appear identical, the layout of the stitch numbers is quite different.

As with other crosses of this nature, the movements 2 and 3 create an overlap of stitches, one coming over and appearing larger than the other.

In the second sample shown on page 32 a subtle change has been made in the crosses to create evenly sized black stitches, thus improving the balance of the design.

In this example four sequences of moves are made with the cross as shown. This is followed by four sequences of moves made with the cross reversed.

Movement 1 is made by lifting the L.H first and the R.H second. Movement 2 is made by lifting R.H first and L.H second.

Continue braiding, changing the order of the cross every four sequences.

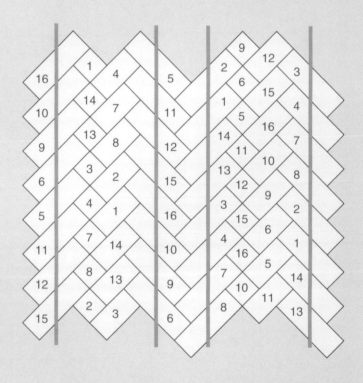

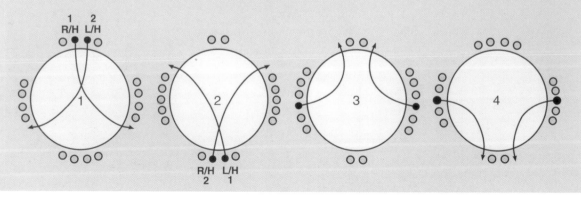

An unusually shaped rectangular braid with a slit in one side.

To keep the edges of the slit close together the threads crossed in movement 3 must be well tensioned.

This can be reaffirmed by tensioning again in movement 4.

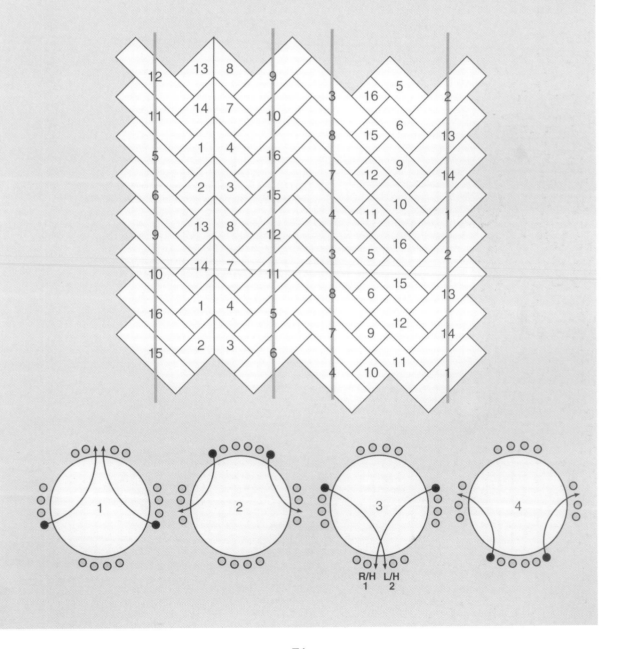

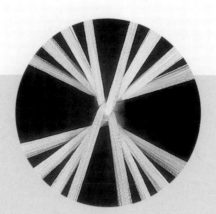

This is a direct expansion of braid 8M and produces a soft, four finned braid. Readjusting for this braid is not easy. Try lifting all the threads from a set of four bobbins across the back of the hand or palm so as to reposition four bobbins with one hand.

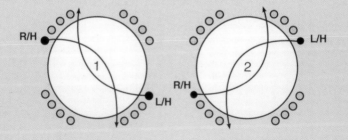

An eight sided braid made from a variation of braid 8M.

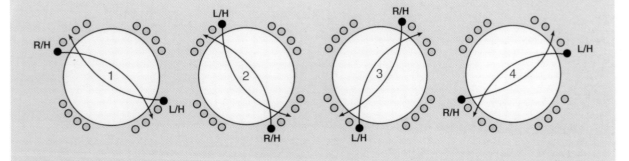

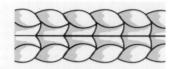

16AC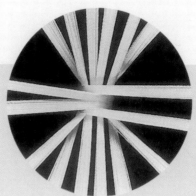

A combination of braid 8D and a variation of braid 8M.

The movements 3 and 4 generate ridges on two faces of the braid.

The ridge can be adjusted to the centre of the faces by rearranging the moves as shown:

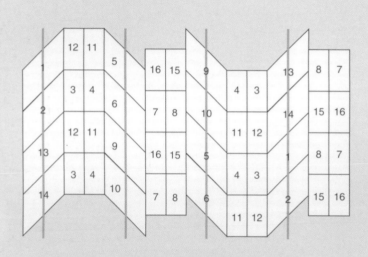

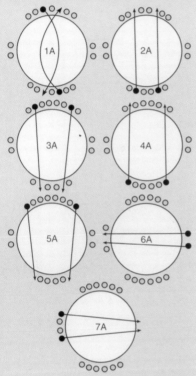

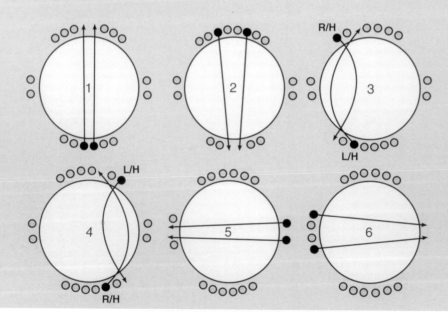

Here braid 4A forms a square inner core with a twelve bobbin version of braid 8M forming four outer ridges.

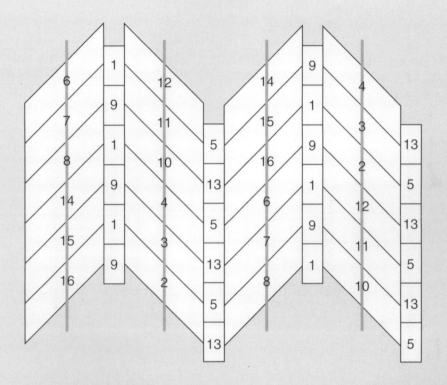

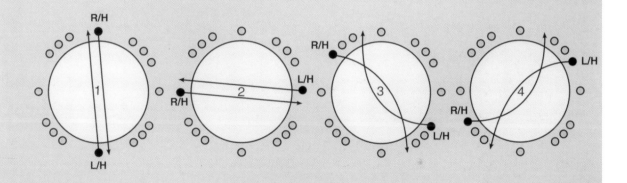

Finishing

As the braiding process draws to a close, take care that the knots joining the warp and the bobbin leaders do not interrupt the flow and rhythm of your work. If you want the braid to end at a specific point, it is always worth doing a few extra sequences to allow for wastage during the finishing process. When the braid has been completed it will be necessary to secure the braid temporarily to stop it from unravelling. This can be done by tying crochet cotton around the braid just below the 'Point of Braiding'. After a more permanent finish has been added, the crochet cotton can be removed

When the braid is secure, lower the weight bag until it rests on the base of the Marudai. Now the bobbins can be removed by pulling the release knot of the cotton leader. Finally, remove the weight bag.

Be aware that as the braid has been made under tension, a certain amount of shrinkage will take place as the braid relaxes.

TASSEL ENDS

The usual procedure at this point is to make tassels with the warp threads at each end of the braid. This is done by sewing with a suitable thread into the braid at a point where the braid will end and the tassel begin.

Then whip smoothly over the sewing by winding the thread round and round the braid. End with a couple of neat stitches into the braid side of the whipping. Loosen any braiding stitches left in the tassel side of the whipping. If winding method 1 has been used, the first section of braid will need to be unravelled to form the tassel. The ends can now be steamed over a kettle to straighten them, which will also help to remove kinks and 'set' the braid. To achieve an evenly cut tassel, roll the tassel threads in a small piece of straight edged paper. Trim the threads close to the ends of this paper tube.

Photograph 21: Cutting a neat tassel.

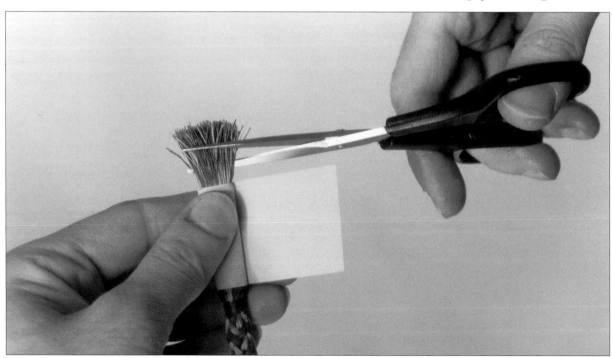

Better results are achieved by using threads that have not been braided. So if you wish to leave a tassel using winding method 1, an extra tie must be added at the warping stage. When the wound bobbins are all hanging from the post and have been tied together, add an extra knot with some crochet cotton. This should be tied around all the threads and at a short distance down the warp.

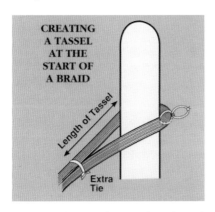

This will result in the braid starting at the extra tie, leaving a length of warp unbraided.

LARGER TASSELS

Once a tassel has been made, its size can be increased by the addition of extra threads:

1) Using the same threads as in the warp, make a group of short lengths. Tie them tightly together in the centre. This can be done by wrapping the threads around a piece of suitably sized card. Tie the threads together at one edge and cut them along the other.

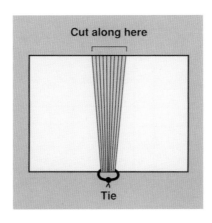

2) Divide the group of threads as shown.

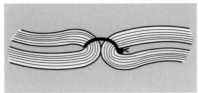

3) Now divide the braid tassel in two. Lay the extra threads across the centre of the braid at right angles to the braid tassel. Sew down securely before steaming and trimming.

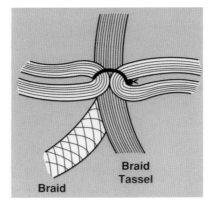

It is possible to make a feature of the tasselled end by using a contrasting colour for the additional tassel threads or the whipped end. *For example, see photograph 27 (top).*

BLUNT ENDS

When using winding method 1, a blunt end will have been created at the start. However this is a 'false' blunt end as the removal of the cotton will cause the braid to unravel. This can be overcome by replacing the crochet cotton with some compatible thread and carefully sewing in, such as the blunt end, *shown in photograph 27 (centre).*

Obviously the neater the layout and work at the start of the braid, the better the final result.

To make a blunt end at the finish of a braid is not easy, as the threads need to be sewn back into the braids as neatly as possible. Hollow braids are perhaps the most suitable, as the thread from each bobbin can be hidden inside the braid and a few, well-placed stitches can hold them all secure. Unfortunately it will change the feel and thickness at this point and is something to be considered when looking at the design and function of the final piece.

TRUE BLUNT ENDS

The decision to make a true blunt end needs to be made before winding the warp. The warp threads need to be connected to two bobbins, one at each end, so that when work starts, they interlock and the braid is prevented from unravelling *(see example photograph 37, top right).*

As the bobbins need to be wound in pairs, colour combinations using even numbers will have to be used. Winding for blunt ends is similar to winding method 2 *(see page 10),* however, the distance between the posts must be full distance. Wind the threads for two bobbins at a time, the thread wound from A to B being for one bobbin; the thread wound from B to A for the other bobbin. Tie off with crochet cotton on **both** sides before continuing to wind for the next pair. When all the threads have been wound between the posts, tie them together very tightly at post 'B', making an extra loop in the cotton for the chopstick. Cut all the threads at post 'A'. The warp can then be brought to the Marudai and the bobins attached.

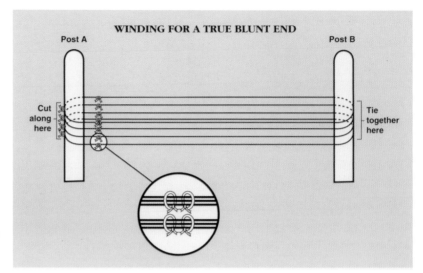

The layout of the bobbins before braiding should be given some thought as it will affect the form of the blunt end. It may help to loosen the central tie to see the thread layout more easily. For example, in braid 8F, the threads can be arranged in adjacent pairs to produce a hollow end or arranged in opposite pairs to produce a solid end *(see diagram below).*

Hollow blunt ends can themselves be very useful as a new form of finishing. Braid ends can disappear into the hollow end, thus hiding the finishing threads. 'Continuous' braids can be made in this manner with the end of a braid disappearing into its beginning. Careful matching and sewing can conceal the join reasonably effectively *(see photograph 22).*

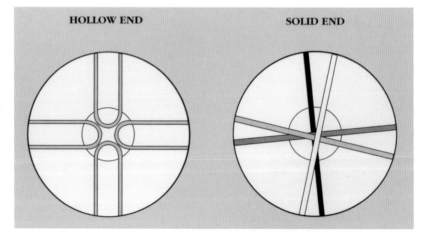

Photograph 22 (opposite): Orchids with braid frame (see page 100).

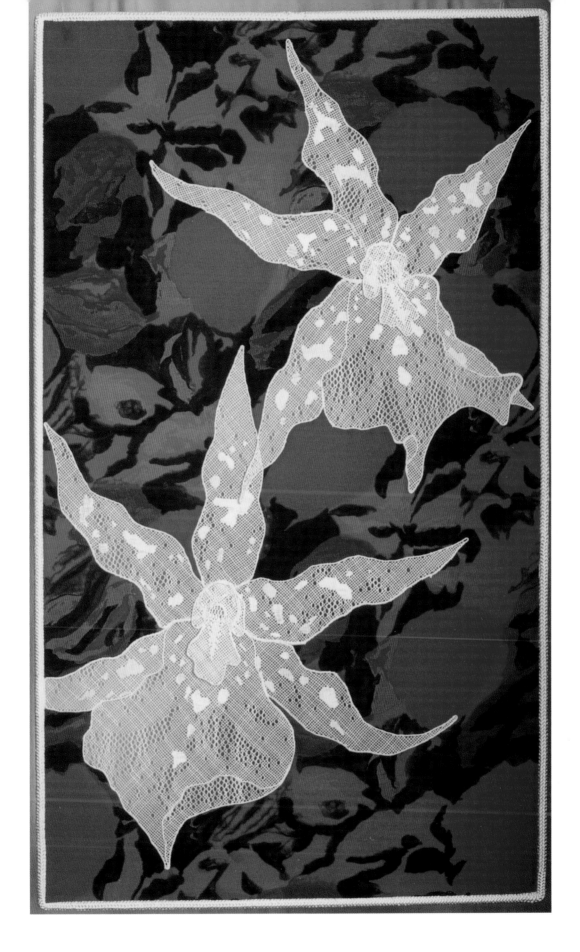

79

LOOPED ENDS

WHIPPED LOOPS

Sometimes looped ends are a design requirement. The easiest way to do this is to fold the braid back on itself. Sew the braid together and make an extended whipping over the join.

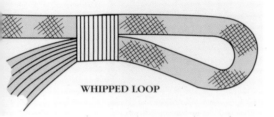

WHIPPED LOOP

If you wish to trim the ends to remove the tassel, ensure that the whipping and sewing are suitably tight. Another option is to cover the join using an idea from the next section.

BUTTONHOLE LOOP

As with the blunt ends, a more structurally sound loop needs to be started at the point of winding the warp. The easiest option is to wind the bobbins using the method for blunt ends (see page 78). When the bobbins have all been wound, use one bobbin to make buttonhole stitches over half of the warp. Remember to wind extra thread on this bobbin to allow for the take up. Work from the central cotton tie, out to a suitable distance. Temporarily tie both ends of the buttonholing together, forming the loop. Braiding will secure the loop permanently.

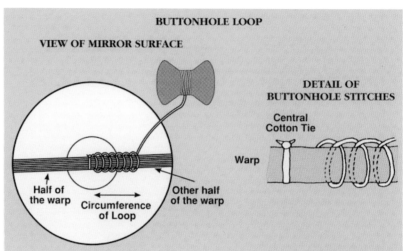

BUTTONHOLE LOOP

VIEW OF MIRROR SURFACE

Half of the warp

Circumference of Loop

Other half of the warp

DETAIL OF BUTTONHOLE STITCHES

Central Cotton Tie

Warp

BRAIDED LOOP

Alternatively, when the warp is ready, only attach bobbins to one half of the warp. Take care that the thread does not slip through the central cotton tie.

Push the other half of the warp down through the central hole of the Marudai. Use the wound bobbins to braid a small section. This will be a 4 bobbin braid, or an 8 bobbin, depending on whether the final braid uses 8 or 16 bobbins. Do not forget to alter the weight bag accordingly.

When a suitable amount of braid has been made, pass the remaining warp back through the hole and attach the rest of the bobbins. Use a cotton tie to temporarily hold the loop until the braiding interlocks it in place.

Photograph 23: Looped ends.
Top: Braided loop.
Middle: Button-hole loop.
Bottom: Whipped loop.

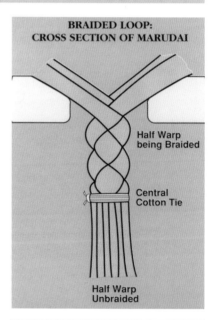

BRAIDED LOOP: CROSS SECTION OF MARUDAI

Half Warp being Braided

Central Cotton Tie

Half Warp Unbraided

JAPANESE LOOP

A more traditional approach is as follows:

Wind the warp for a blunt end. Take the threads for just two bobbins and tie them together at post 'B'. Cut them at post 'A' and remove them from the remaining warp.

Attach this part warp to the Marudai in the usual fashion. Taking the thread intended for just one bobbin, split into 4. This will probably influence your initial choice of threads per bobbin.

Attach 4 bobbins to the split threads. Push the remaining threads through the mirror's central hole.

Braid a small section of 4A. When this is complete, secure the braid with crochet cotton and remove the bobbins. Sew the braided section together to form a loop. You now have the thread for 2 bobbins with a small braided loop at their centre. Allow these threads to re-join the main warp and continue as normal. Remember that the 'take-up' of this method will not be standard.

COVERED ENDS

The ends of the braids can be covered or inserted into any number of different objects of various materials (metal, wood, ceramic, plastic etc.), providing there is an accommodating hole into which the braid can fit. One such example is the use of metal bell-

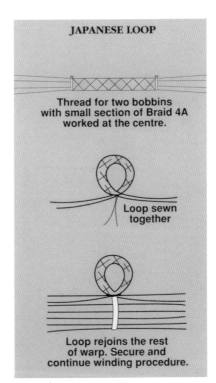

JAPANESE LOOP

Thread for two bobbins with small section of Braid 4A worked at the centre.

Loop sewn together

Loop rejoins the rest of warp. Secure and continue winding procedure.

caps for jewellery. To attach the braid to a bell-cap, first make a strong neat sewing and whip over the top. Carefully trim the threads close to the whipping. Then, using a suitable adhesive, fix the end of the braid into the bell-cap.

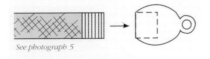

See photograph 5

Where appropriate this method can be used to join braids to larger objects, so that the braid becomes an attached feature. Ends can also be hidden in fabric either by losing the end of the braid into a seam of a large fabric piece or as shown in photograph 27 (bottom), by covering the braid end with fabric.

BEADED ENDS

Beads can be used as a decorative feature on braid ends, such as the gold beads sewn on the padded tassel in photograph 25. They can also be used as a covered end such as the example shown in photograph 24 (inset). The braid is attached inside the bead using the same method as shown previously.

The example in photograph 24 shows a beaded tassel which provides a weightier end than a thread tassel. Here a 'skirt' of beads is sewn around the braid end.

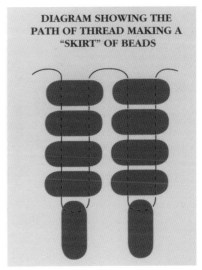

DIAGRAM SHOWING THE PATH OF THREAD MAKING A "SKIRT" OF BEADS

OTHER FANCY ENDINGS

In addition to the above, there are a multitude of other finishes, far too many to be covered in this book. However, there follows a few examples to illustrate.

Photograph 24, Beaded Ends. (See page 81 & 100)

Photograph 25, Covered Ball Ends. (See page 84 & 100)

SPLIT ENDS

Before arriving at the end of the warp, secure the braid and remove the bobbins. Divide the threads that were on one bobbin into 4. Add bobbins to each division and work a 4A braid to the end. Do not forget to adjust the content of the weight bag. Secure this braid and repeat for all the remaining thread for each bobbin.

The example shown in photograph 27 (top right) is for braid 16G. It divides into four 4A braids. No securing is needed for this split as the braid moves hold the threads in place. Each 4A braid is secured, then sixteen 4A braids are worked using the divided threads from each bobbin.

KNOTTED ENDS

Many different knots can be added to braid ends. The example, right, is a Chinese ball knot. At a calculates point the braid changes from 8H to 8K. When braiding is complete a Chinese ball knot is tied at the pattern change-over point. The end of the braid is secured by sewing within the knot structure.

COVERED BALLS

A ball of wadding is sewn at the centre of the tassel and the threads carefully arranged around it. A new tassel is created under the ball and sewn in place. The ball can then be covered, in these examples in photograph 25, by sewing open work button-hole stitch-es and by couched threads and beads.

DIRECT ATTACHMENT

The warp threads can be attached to objects before braiding commences. In exam-ple photograph 27 (top left) each bobbin is attached to the keyring by making a larks head knot with the warp threads. When all the bobbins are attached, the weight bag can be hung from the keyring and braiding commenced.

Photograph 26: Knotted ends (see page 100)

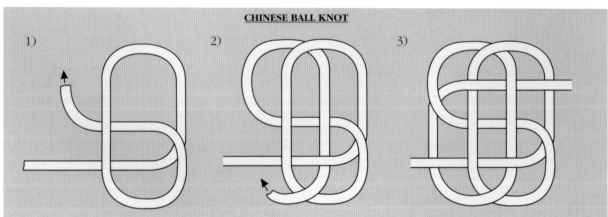

CHINESE BALL KNOT

1)

2)

3)

84

Photograph 27: Various endings. Top Left: Direct attachment (see pages 84 & 100). Top Right: Split ends (see pages 81 & 100). Bottom: Covered ends (see pages 81 & 100).

Creative Effects

Kumihimo is a very adaptable technique. The lack of restriction creates a wealth of potential waiting to be explored. It is simply a matter of understanding the cause and effect of this technique. Even mistakes, which feel like a great burden to the beginner, should be lessons to relish as they can be developed into new exciting pieces.

For example, a common error whilst working braid 8F is for these moves to be made instead of movement 1.

This, however, can be used to great effect when 'errors' are added at regular intervals *(see photograph 28, below)*. The examples that follow are just a few ideas of the endless possibilities intended **for those who have an understanding of the basic braid structures** already covered.

Photograph 28: Zig-zags (see page 98).

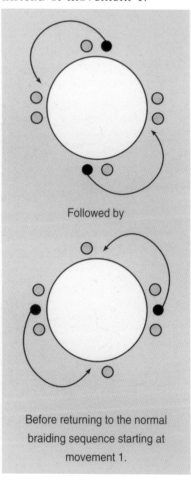

Followed by

Before returning to the normal braiding sequence starting at movement 1.

Photograph 29: Casket (see page 87).

HOLLOW BRAIDS

16N is the most obvious hollow braid but many others have this potential. The hollowness of a braid can be exaggerated by the use of a 'former'. This is usually a wooden stick around which the braid is made. As braiding is completed, it is removed leaving an empty space within the braid structure. However, braids can be made using more permanent filling such as in the framework for the casket *(see photograph 29)*. In this case braid 16P was worked around metal rods resulting in a solid braid that was strong enough to create a structure to support the lace work.

Passive threads can also be braided around in the same manner. They can be simply extra padding for the braid, lying dormant within the structure, or can be interchanged with warp threads at specific points to change the character of the braid being worked.

To actually work these ideas, an overhead support is required. This can be a bar, or a hook, secured from the ceiling or from the sides and positioned directly over the Marudai. String is hung over the support, one end attached to a counter-balance weight, the other to the former, or passive threads thus keeping them in an upright position above the point of braiding. The counter-balance should be light enough to allow the former, or threads, to descend slowly as they are braided around. Do make sure the weight bag is firmly attached, providing tension on the inner core as well as on the outer threads.

A word of warning to those wishing to braid around metal rods. Remember that the completed braid will be unable to bend when it reaches the base of the Marudai, therefore extended legs may be needed.

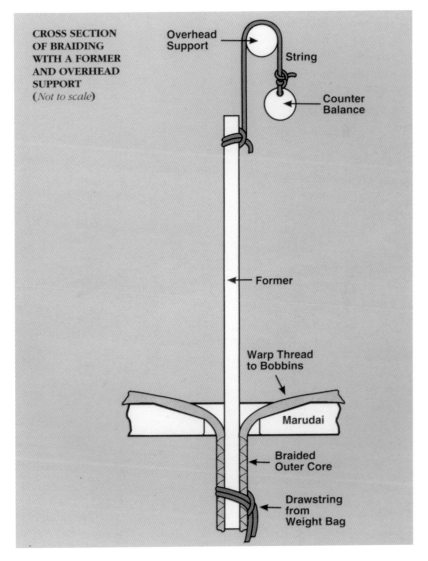

CROSS SECTION OF BRAIDING WITH A FORMER AND OVERHEAD SUPPORT (*Not to scale*)

Overhead Support

String

Counter Balance

Former

Warp Thread to Bobbins

Marudai

Braided Outer Core

Drawstring from Weight Bag

EXAMPLE 1
Photograph 30 (below)

In this example a warp of twelve bobbins is wound, although it is always braid 8F that is worked. Six bobbins are loaded with black, two with red, two with orange and two with rust. Initially eight bobbins are arranged around the mirror in this order:

Bobbin numbers 1, 3, 4, 5, 7 and 8 are black. Bobbin numbers 2 and 6 are red. The four remaining bobbins are hung from the support bar to form the inner core.

As the threads are already attached to weighted bobbins, no counter-balance is required.

Wadding, or in this case small polystyrene balls, are added in the core to create bulges in the hollow braid. Care is needed to get the stitches lieing evenly around the sphere. It may help to sew, or tie, the ball in place to stop it rising above the point of braiding.

When the ball is covered the bobbins on the support bar are swapped so that four black bobbins are now passive and the colour layout on the mirror is as follows:

Bobbin numbers 1 and 5 are black. Bobbin numbers 2 and 6 are red. Bobbin numbers 3 and 7 are rust. Bobbin numbers 4 and 8 are orange.

After a short length of braid 8F the bobbins are swapped back to their original positions and another ball is added. As soon as the ball is covered, the second layout is used again to produce a long length of braid with intermittent changes. These are produced with a colour layout as follows:

Bobbin numbers 1, 3, 4, 5, 7 and 8 are black. Bobbin number 2 is red. Bobbin number 6 is orange.

This leaves two rust, one red and one orange passive on the support bar.

The braid is ended with the addiiton of two more balls worked in the same manner as the two others.

When the braid is complete, each interchange is whipped in black thread to secure the balls and to disguise any irregularities. Black threads are cut out of the tassel and extra coloured threads added as shown on page 77.

Photograph 30: Hollow braid (Example 1).

FLOATING THREADS

This occurs when certain bobbins 'rest' whilst the others continue braiding. When the bobbins come back into play a 'float' is created over the continued braid.

(Some examples of floating thread have already been illustrated in Chapter 4, e.g. braid 16P and its variation).

Any number and position of bobbins can 'rest' and their point of return into work does not have to be from the same point from which they left. This is shown in the following examples:

EXAMPLE 1
Photograph 31 (left).
This is worked with initial colour layout:
Bobbin numbers 1, 2, 5, 6, 9, 10, 13 and 14 are blue.
Bobbin numbers 3, 4, 11 and 12 are gold.
Bobbin numbers 7, 8, 15 and 16 are black.
One sequence of braid 16J is worked. The second sequence omits movements 1 & 2 allowing the gold bobbins to rest. By moving these bobbins to a new position the angle of the float is changed.

The gold bobbins must be taken to their new position **under** the adjacent bobbin threads.

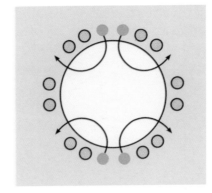

Another full sequence of braid 16J is now worked. This is followed by a sequence that omits movements 5 & 6. The floating gold bobbins are now returned to the centre **under** the adjacent bobbins ready for the whole procedure to be repeated.

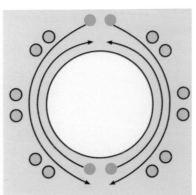

Variations of this procedure are endless and can include floats made without allowing bobbins to rest, as in the following example.

EXAMPLE 2
Photograph 31 (middle)
The initial colour layout is as follows:
Bobbin numbers 1, 2, 9 and 10 are gold.
Bobbin numbers 3, 4, 7, 8, 11, 12, 15 and 16 are blue.
Bobbin numbers 5, 6, 13 and 14 are black.

In this example braid 16E is worked. Before each sequence the gold bobbin positions are changed by going **under** all the other threads.

Remember to make each cross-over uniform. In this case the two top bobbins go outside the ones coming up from the bottom.

Photograph 31: Floating Threads. Examples 1,2 &3 (left to right)

EXAMPLE 3

Photograph 31 (right)

Another possibility is to create floats by using passive threads from within a hollow braid. Here braid 16F is worked around four passive gold threads that are supported above the point of braiding *(as shown on page 87)*. The external crosses are created at set intervals by bringing down the gold threads to lie in these positions.

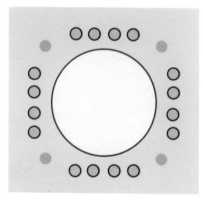

Two sequences are worked of 16F. The gold threads are not included in these moves. Now cross the gold threads **under** the threads of the North and South sets of bobbins.

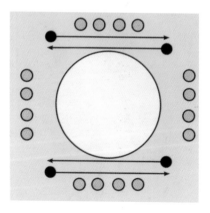

Then cross them over the West and East bobbins.

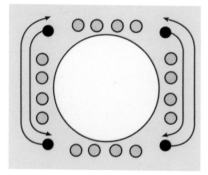

Work two sequences of 16F. Now cross the gold bobbins **under** the West and East sets of bobbins and **over** the North and South sets.

Work another two sequences of 16F. Finally cross the golds **under** North and South sets and return to passive upward position.

EXAMPLE 4

Photograph 38

Tufted braids are another interesting feature that can be created using floating threads. Providing the braid is tightly woven and the threads have suitable friction, floating threads can be cut to form tufts that are held in place by the remaining stitches in the braid.

The following example shows one sequence that creates floats sufficiently woven within the braid to remain secure when cut.

Work sequence braid 8A with twelve bobbins. The four extra bobbins will be the ones that make the tufts. These are

placed around the Marudai as shown:

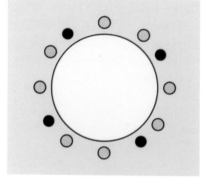

Two extra moves are required:

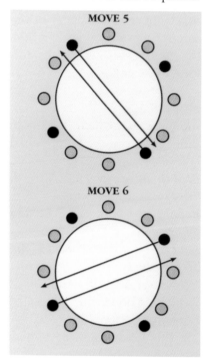

Work the sequence with moves as follows:
1, 2, 3, 4.
1, 2, 3, 4.
5, 6.
1, 2, 3, 4.
5, 6.
The large floats can now be cut in half to form two tufts.

DISTORTED BRAIDS

EXAMPLE 1

Photograph 27 (top)

Floating threads can be pulled tight to distort the braid. In this example work is commenced using braid 16G. Floating threads are created by resting the bobbins numbered 5, 8, 13 and 16. A length of braid 16J is worked with the remaining bobbins (without moves 5 & 6). Now work one sequence of 16G, pulling hard on moves 5 & 6 so that the floating threads become tight. The 16J braid is forced to the side forming a loop. The example is created by varying the number of stitches in the 16J braid and the side to which the loop falls.

EXAMPLE 2

Photograph 32

Braids can also be distorted by the use of unevenly weighted bobbins, or in this case, by uneven tensioning of threads. The example is braid 8G. Bobbin number 1 is pulled hard every time it reaches the edge of the flat braid; this is every fourth sequence. Similar effects can be caused through the use of different threads. When a braid is finished and the threads are no longer under tension, any difference in the shrinkage of the threads can distort the braid.

EXAMPLE 3

Photograph 33

Braid structure can be distorted when the threads are used in different ratios. Examples of this are seen in the photograph.

Here eight bobbins are each wound with ten threads of purple. The other eight bobbins are each wound with forty threads of red.

Braid 16T (top) is made with the thicker threads lying in bobbin positions 1, 7, 8, 10, 11, 12, 13 and 14.

Braid 16U (middle) is made with the thicker threads lying in bobbin positions 5, 6, 7, 8, 13, 14, 15 and 16.

Braid 16B (bottom) is made with the thicker threads lying in bobbin positions 9, 10, 11, 12, 13, 14, 15 and 16.

Photograph 32 (top): Distorted braid, example 2.
Photograph 33 (below): Distorted braid, example 3.

Creative Effects

Photograph 34: Beads, Examples 1 & 2 (left to right).

BEADS

Beads can be successfully combined with finishing braids, as seen in photograph 37 (top). They can also be used as a decorative feature during the braiding process.

EXAMPLE 1
Photograph 34 (left)
Single beads can be threaded onto the individual bobbins at the warping stage. Obviously the size of the hole and the thread thickness need to be compatible. The beads sit on, or near, the bobbin during braiding and are pushed up to the point of braiding when required.

Here, seed beads are added to two bobbins. The order in which the beads are threaded plays an important part in the design.

They are threaded in repeats of grey, pink, grey, mauve on one bobbin and grey, mauve, grey, pink on the other. These 2 loaded bobbins are placed in a starting position of 1 & 5 North and South for braid 8A.

One bead from each bobbin is pushed to the point of braiding at the beginning of every other sequence.

EXAMPLE 2
Photograph 34 (right)
For this example, seed beads were threaded onto 8 bobbins. These are placed around the mirror in starting positions 3, 4, 7, 8, 11, 12, 15 and 16. Braid 16P is worked. The cluster of beads is created by working moves 1 to 4 five times, then push 5 seed beads from each bobbin to the point of braiding. Secure the beads with moves 5A, 6A, 7A and 8A from the variation of braid 16P (see page 61). As the five beads are longer than the five sequences of braid, they curve outward to form a ball shape. Continue with 16P until the next cluster is required.

EXAMPLE 3
Photograph 37 (bottom right)
Strings of beads can be used in place of threads on a bobbin. In the examples semi-precious beads were wound on one bobbin and worked with braiding sequence 8F. Care must be taken with the weight bag tension if the threads are to lie evenly between each bead.

As the beads are worked into the braid they gradually force the remaining beads along the string. For this reason the beads should be threaded onto an extra long string that is secured with a release knot. As the beads tighten, the pressure can be released by frequently re-tieing the knot further down the beading string.

HOLES

The most obvious method to create holes in a braid is to use braid 8C. The concept of making one braid divided into two braids, before returning to one braid, can be used in various formats.

EXAMPLE 1
Photograph 37 (bottom left)
Shows braid 16D divided into 2 braids of 8D. This can be done by moving the 8D sequence with the bobbins off centre (see diagram right). Work the mirror image moves for the right hand set of 8 bobbins. Repeat sequence as required. In this example, four sequences are worked with each 8D braid before returning to braid 16D. Alternatively, rearrange the bobbins so that a set of 8 are worked from their correct positions. Then interchange to work the other set of 8. Whichever method is used, care must be taken with the tension.

EXAMPLE 2 *Photograph 36*
Hole features can be created using a combination of flat braid 8G and hollow braid 8F. In this example just two sequences of 8F are worked at set points along an 8G braid. This produces eyelets through which smaller 8F braids are threaded to form the lattice work decorating the purse.

EXAMPLE 3 *Photograph 35*
The reverse of Example 2 is to

work one sequence of 8G at intervals on 8F braid. This creates holes in the hollow braid. Here, they reveal the passive inner core of a metal rod.

Photograph 35: Holes, Example 3.

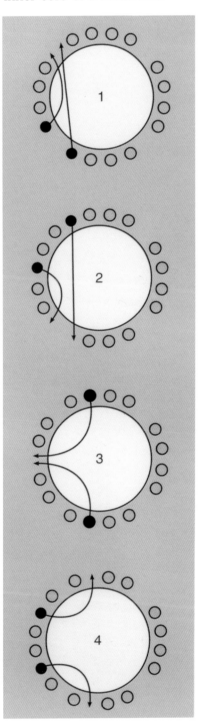

Photograph 36: Purse: Holes, Example 2 (see page 93).

Photograph 37, Top Left: Black onyx necklace (see page 100). Top right: Combined braid, Example 4 (see page 97 & 100). Bottom left: Holes, Example 1 (see page 93 & 100). Bottom right: Beads, Example 3 (see page 92 & 100).

COMBINING BRAIDS

EXAMPLE 1
Photograph 39

Combining finished braids enables the play of colour, pattern, shape and texture to be mixed and explored, resulting in a multitude of possibilities.

The example opposite shows necklaces made with a combination of four braids twisted with a string of semi-precious stones.

EXAMPLE 2
Photograph 12

Braids can also be combined during the braiding process. Previously made braids can be wound onto a bobbin, or bobbins, in place of the threads, and reworked into a new braid.

Initially a gold and red 8F braid is worked using twenty strands of thread on each bobbin. This braid is wound on one bobbin, and is re-braided with seven other bobbins, each loaded with twenty strands of thread.

The structure of the second 8F braid is distorted. This occurs as a result of the size difference between the threads and the braid. If they were similar in size, the distortion would be minimal. The distortion in the example has been increased by reducing the weight in the weight bag.

Photograph 38 (left): Tufted braids (see page 90 & 100)

Photograph 39 (above right): Chokers, a combination of 4 braids and semi-precious stones (see page 100).

EXAMPLE 3
Photograph 6

Braids can be braided back into themselves during their production. Here, braid 16G is worked. At set points during the braiding process, the finished braid is lifted up to lie across the point of braiding, but remaining below the mirror, in this case from East to West. Work is continued, trapping the final braid, thus creating a loop. Note that the weight bag will be unable to slide up the braid, and it will be necesssary to un-knot the Larks head and retie above the loop.

EXAMPLE 4
Photograph 37 (top right)

Another example of a combined braid. Here, a braid 8F is worked with purple and blue threads. When completed this braid is used as a passive inner core of a red braid 16N. A few sewing stitches may help to keep the 8F braid in place inside the blunt end of the 16N braid. The 16N braid is worked around the 8F braid. After a short distance make a tight, temporary tie around braid 16N. Pull the warp and braid 8F down through the central hole of the mirror and make another tie at a set distance above the other tie. These ties enable braiding to be resumed at a point further up braid 8F. Make a number of ties as required. When braid 16N is complete replace the ties with permanent whipped ends and trim the red threads to expose the braid 8F.

The initial colour layout is given for each example. The bobbin starting position numbers referred to can be found on page 26.

Photograph 1. Combined Braids.
Details of combined braids on page 97. First braid 8F is worked with 20 strands of silk on each bobbin. Bobbins 1, 2, 5, 6 are green and bobbins 3, 4, 7, 8 are red. The final braid 8G is made with the first braid on bobbin No. 1. The other 7 bobbins ar each loaded with 10 strands of blue and 10 strands of purple silk.

Photograph 3. Unusual Threads.
Braid 8A: bobbins 1, 3 are ruched ribbon. Bobbins 2, 4, 5, 6, 7, 8 are mixed blue and purple silk. The braid finishes with braid 4A worked in the silk. The other threads are sewn in at the change over point.

Photograph 4. Distorted Braids.
TOP: Braid 16B worked with:
Bobbins 1, 2, 9, 10 are 20 strands of cream silk.
Bobbins 3, 4, 11, 12 are 12 strands of yellow silk.
Bobbins 5, 6, 13, 14 are 6 strands of brown silk.
Bobbins 7, 8, 15, 16 are 3 strands of red silk.

MIDDLE:
Braid 16T worked with:
Bobbins 1 to 8 are 16 strands of brown silk.
Bobbins 9 to 16 are 4 strands of red silk.

BOTTOM:
Braid 16D worked with:
Bobbins 1, 4, 5, 8, 9, 12, 13, 16 are 16 strands of yellow silk.
Bobbins 2, 3, 6, 7, 10, 11, 14, 15 are 4 strands of red silk.

Distorted braids are discussed on page 91. The hand-turned brass ends illustrated are an example of covered ends detailed on page 81.

Photograph 5. Bell Caps.
Braid 16N: Worked around a shaped former. Fitted into brass bell-caps. Details on page 81.

Photograph 6. Combined Braid Example 3.
Braid 16G: Bobbins 1, 4, 10, 11 are bright green.

Bobbins 2, 3, 9, 12 are olive.
Bobbins 5, 6, 7, 8, 13, 14, 15, 16 are black.
Working details are given on page 97.

Photograph 7. Difference in weight bag tension.
Braid 16U: Bobbins 1, 2, 3, 4, 7, 8, 13, 14 are cream.
Bobbins 5, 6, 15, 16 are red.
Bobbins 9, 10, 11, 12 are brown.

Photograph 9. Shell Bag.
A silk lace and embroidered bag with matching braid handle, a combined braid (see page 97). The first braid is 8F worked with all the bobbins in course silk. The final braid 8F has the first braid on bobbin 1. Bobbins 2 and 6 are loaded with course silk and the rest of the bobbins each loaded with a mix of soft pearly silk.

Photograph 10. Pattern Changes.
All braid 8F. Initial colour layouts from top to bottom.
1. *Bobbins 2, 5, 6 are black.*
   Bobbins 1, 3, 4, 7, 8 are white.
2. *Bobbins 1, 3, 4, 5, 7, 8 are black.*
   Bobbins 2, 6 are white.
3. *Bobbin 1 is black.*
   Bobbins 2 to 8 are white.
4. *Bobbins 2, 4, 5, 6, 7, 8 are black.*
   Bobbins 1, 3 are white.
5. *Bobbins 1, 2, 3, 4 are black.*
   Bobbins 5, 6, 7, 8 are white.
6. *Bobbins 1, 3, 5 are black.*
   Bobbins 2, 4, 6, 7, 8 are white.
7. *Bobbins 1, 2, 3, 6 are black.*
   Bobbins 4, 5, 7, 8 are white.
8. *Bobbins 1, 3, 5, 7 are black.*
   Bobbins 2, 4, 6, 8 are white.
9. *Bobbins 1, 2, 5, 6 are black.*
   Bobbins 3, 4, 7, 8 are white.

Photograph 11. Structure Changes.
Braids made of string using sequences from left to right: 8H, 16T, 16D, 16P, 16E, 16B & 16Q. The first four are worked around a wooden former that remains inside the braid.
Formers are discussed on page 87.

Photograph 12. Combined Braid Example 2.
Initial colour layout of the first braid is:
Bobbins 1, 2, 5, 6 are red.
Bobbins 3, 4, 7, 8 are gold.
The final braid has an initial layout of bobbin 1, loaded with the first braid.
Bobbins 2, 6 are black.

Bobbins 3, 4, 7, 8 are blue.
Bobbin 5 is burgundy.
Working details are given on page 97.

Photograph 13. Chinese Knot.
A Chinese good luck knot tied with braid 8H: Bobbins 1, 4, 5, 8 are black.
Bobbins 2, 3, 6, 7 are yellow.

Photograph 14. Braids in use.
CAMISOLE TOP:
Shoulder straps and waist tie of braid 8F: Bobbins 1, 3, 4, 7, 8 are black.
Bobbin 5 is a mix of pink and mauve.
Bobbins 2, 6 are a mix of red and gold.

PAISLEY SHAWL:
A 16 bobbin version of the variation of braid 8A (see page 34). Expansion is achieved by increasing the number of moves. This is method 2 described on page 22.

Photograph 15. *Top to Bottom.*
Braid 4A: 1, 3 are grey. 2 is green, 4 is burgundy.
Braid 4A: 1, 2 are yellow. 3, 4 are brown.
Braid 8A: 1, 5, 6, 7, 8 are black. 2, 4 are green. 3 is light green
Braid 8A (variation): 1, 3, 7 are yellow. 2, 4, 6, 8 are green. 5 is burgundy.
Braid 8B: 1, 5 are yellow. 2, 6 are cream. 3, 4, 7, 8 are black.
Braid 8B: 1, 5 are yellow. 2, 3, 4 are burgundy. 6, 7, 8 are green.
Braid 8C: 1, 3, 5, 7 are burgundy. 2, 4, 6, 8 are grey.
Braid 8C (variation): 1, 4, 5, 8 are yellow. 2, 3, 6, 7 are cream.
Braid 8D: 1, 2, 3, 8 are grey. 4, 5, 6, 7 are burgundy.
Braid 8D: 1, 2 are cream. 3, 4, 7, 8 are brown. 5, 6 are yellow.
Braid 8E: 1, 4, 6, 7 are green. 2, 3, 5, 8 are light green.
Braid 8E: 1, 2, 3, 4 are yellow. 5, 6, 7, 8 are burgundy.
Braid 8F: 1, 3, 4, 7, 8 are black. 2, 5, 6 are light green.
Braid 8F: 1 is black, 3 is burgundy, 5 is green. 2, 4, 6, 7, 8 are yellow.

Photograph 16. *Bottom to top.*
Braid 8G: 1, 3, 5, 7 are pink. 2, 4, 6, 8 are burgundy.
Braid 8G: 1, 8 are purple. 2, 3 are red. 4, 5, 6, 7 are blue.
Braid 8H: 1, 4, 5, 7, 8 are black. 2, 6 are pink, 3 is burgundy.
Braid 8H: 1, 2 are purple. 3, 8 are blue. 4, 7 are mauve, 5, 6 are light blue.

Braid 8J: 1, 2, 5, 6 are red. 3, 4, 7, 8 are blue.

Braid 8J: 1, 3, 5, 7 are black. 2, 4, 6, 8 are burgundy.

Braid 8K: 1, 5, 6, 7, 8 are red. 2, 4 are purple, 3 is blue.

Braid 8K: 1, 2, 4, 7 are purple. 3, 8 are mauve. 5, 6 are blue.

Braid 8L: 1, 6, 7, 8 are pink. 2, 3, 4, 5 are blue.

Braid 8L: 1, 2, 3, 4, 7, 8 are red. 5, 6 are black.

Braid 8M: 3, 4, 7, 8 are black. 1 is mauve, 2 is light blue. 5 is blue, 6 is purple.

Braid 8M: 1, 3, 5, 6 are pink. 2, 4, 7, 8 are burgundy.

Braid 8N: 1, 2 are mauve. 3, 4, 7, 8 are blue. 5, 6 are light blue.

Braid 8N: 1, 2 are red. 3, 6, 8 are purple. 4, 5, 7 are blue.

Photograph 17. *Top to Bottom.*
Braid 16A: 1 to 8 are black. 9 to 16 are green.

Braid 16A: 1, 4, 9, 12 are brown. 2, 3, 10, 11 are light brown. 5, 8, 13, 16 are mustard. 6, 7, 14, 15 are yellow.

Braid 16B: 1, 2, 5, 6, 9, 10, 13, 14 are light green. 3, 4, 11, 12 are green. 7, 8, 15, 16 are black.

Braid 16B: 1 is light green. 2, 3, 7, 8, 14, 15, 16 are white. 4, 5, 6, 9, 13 are black. 10, 11, 12 are green.

Braid 16C: 1, 2, 5, 6, 11, 12 are black. 3, 4, 9, 10, 13, 14 are green. 7, 8, 15, 16 are cream.

Braid 16C: 1, 3, 9, 11 are yellow. 2, 10 are light brown. 4, 5, 6, 12, 13, 14 are white. 7, 8, 15, 16 are brown.

Braid 16D: 1, 7, 9, 15 are light green. 2, 8, 10, 16 are green. 3, 4, 5, 6, 11, 12, 13, 14 are black.

Braid 16D: 1, 4 are cream, 2, 3 are yellow. 5, 6, 7, 8, 13, 14, 15, 16 are black. 9, 12 are light brown, 10, 11 are brown.

Braid 16E: 1, 2, 5, 6, 9, 10, 13, 14 are green. 3, 4, 15, 16 are cream. 7, 8, 11, 12 are white.

Braid 16E (variation): 1, 2, 5, 6, 9, 10, 13, 14 are brown. 3, 4, 7, 8, 11, 12, 15, 16 are yellow.

Braid 16F: 1, 2, 3, 4, 9, 10, 11, 12 are green. 5, 6, 7, 8 are yellow. 13, 14, 15, 16 are black.

Braid 16F (variation): 1, 2, 3, 4, 5, 8, 13, 16 are green. 6, 7, 9, 10, 11, 12, 14, 15 are light green.

Braid 16G: 1, 4, 6, 7, 9, 12, 14, 15 are yellow. 2, 3, 5, 8, 10, 11, 13, 16 are black.

Braid 16G: 1, 4 are green. 2, 3, 6, 7, 9, 12, 14, 15 are black. 5, 8, 13, 16 are dark green. 10, 11 are light green.

Photograph 18. *Bottom to Top.*
Braid 16H: 1, 3, 4 , 6 are red. 2, 5, 9 to 16 are pink. 7, 8 are purple.

Braid 16H: 1, 6, 9, 14 are black. 2, 5, 10, 13 are purple. 3, 4, 11, 12 are grey. 7, 8, 15, 16 are red.

Braid 16J: 1 to 8, 15, 16 are crimson. 9, 10, 13, 14 are grey. 11, 12 are pink.

Braid 16 J (variation): 1, 6, 9, 10, 13, 14 are crimson. 2, 3, 4, 5, 7, 8, 11, 12, 15, 16 are black.

Braid 16K: 1, 2, 5, 6, 9, 10, 13, 14 are purple. 3, 4, 7, 8, 11, 12, 15, 16 are pink.

Braid 16K (variation): 1 to 6 & 9 to 14 are purple. 7, 8, 15, 16 are white.

Braid 16L: 1, 8, 9, 16 are purple. 2, 7, 10, 15 are pink. 3, 6, 11, 14 are light pink. 4, 5, 12, 13 are grey.

Braid 16L: 1, 16 are black. 2, 15 are grey. 3, 14 are purple. 4 to 13 are pink.

Braid 16M: 1, 2, 3, 4, 9, 10, 11, 12 are mauve. 5, 6, 15, 16 are black. 7, 8, 13, 14 are purple.

Braid 16M: 1, 4, 6, 8, 10, 11, 13, 15 are black. 2, 3, 5, 7, 9, 12, 14, 16 are crimson.

Braid 16N: 1 to 4 & 9 to 12 are black. 5 to 8 & 13 to 16 are pink.

Braid 16N: 1, 2, 5, 6, 8, 9, 10, 13, 14, 16 are purple. 3, 7, 11, 15 are mauve. 4, 12 are white.

Braid 16P: 1, 3, 5, 7, 9, 11, 13, 15 are black. 2, 6, 10, 14 are pink. 4, 8, 12, 16 are crimson.

Braid 16P (variation): 1, 2, 5, 6, 9, 10, 13, 14 are crimson. 3, 4, 7, 8, 11, 12 are mauve. 15, 16 are purple.

Photograph 19. *Bottom to Top.*
Braid 16Q: 1, 2, 5, 6, 9, 10, 13, 14 are blue. 3, 4, 7, 11, 12, 15 are cream. 8, 16 are purple.

Braid 16Q (variation): 1, 2, 13, 14 are dark blue. 3, 4, 7, 8, 11, 12, 15, 16 are purple. 5, 6, 9, 10 are blue.

Braid 16R: 1, 2, 7, 8, 9, 10, 15, 16 are white. 3, 4, 11, 12 are mauve. 5, 6, 13, 14 are purple.

Braid 16R: 1, 2, 15, 16 are light blue. 3, 4, 5, 6, 11, 12, 13, 14 are grey. 7, 8, 9, 10 are blue.

Braid 16S: 1, 14 are white. 2 to 13 are purple. 15, 16 are grey.

Braid 16S: 1, 2, 3, 4, 5, 7, 9, 10, 11, 12, 13, 15 are cream. 6, 14 are dark blue. 8, 16 are blue.

Braid 16T: 1, 2, 5, 6, 9, 10, 13, 14 are blue. 3, 4, 11, 12 are grey. 7, 8, 15, 16 are light blue.

Braid 16T: 1, 3, 5, 7, 9, 11, 13, 15 are purple. 2, 8, 10, 16 are blue. 4, 6, 12, 14 are mauve.

Braid 16U: 1, 4 are blue. 2, 3, & 7 to 14 are mauve. 5, 6, 15, 16 are light blue.

Braid 16U: 1, 4 are purple. 2, 3 are blue. 5, 6, 9, 10, 11, 12, 15, 16 are white. 7, 14 are mauve. 8, 13 are light blue.

Braid 16V: 1 to 4, & 7 to 14 are blue. 5, 16 are cream. 6, 15 are light blue.

Braid 16V: 1 to 4 are grey. 5, 6, 9, 10, 11, 12, 15, 16 are purple. 7, 8, 13, 14 are mauve.

Braid 16W: 1, 2, 7, 8, 9, 10, 15, 16 are dark blue. 3, 4, 5, 6, 11, 12, 13, 14 are blue.

Braid 16W: 1, 2, & 11 to 16 are blue. 3, 4, 9, 10 are cream. 5 to 8 are purple.

Photograph 20. *Top to Bottom.*
Braid 16X: 1, 4 are black. 2, 3, 5, 6, 7, 9, 12, 14, 15, 16 are copper. 8, 13 are grey. 10, 11 are crimson.

Braid 16X: 1 to 4, & 9 to 12 are black. 5 to 8, & 13 to 16 are grey.

Braid 16Y: 1, 4, 5, 16 are dark brown. 6, 9, 10, 11, 12, 15 are light brown. 3, 13, 14 are red. 2, 7, 8 are black.

Braid 16Y: (variation): 1, 9, 14, 16 are black. 2 to 8, & 11 to 15 are red. 10 is peach.

Braid 16Z: 1 to 4 are crimson. 5, 6, 9, 10, 11, 12, 15, 16 are black. 7, 8, 13, 14 are brown.

Braid 16Z: 1, 4, 5, 16 are red. 2, 3 are peach. 6 to 15 are grey.

Braid 16AA: 1, 8, 9, 16 are red. 2, 7, 10, 15 are crimson. 3, 6, 11, 14 are brown. 4, 5, 12, 13 are copper.

Braid 16AA: 1, 13 are black. 2, 14 are grey. 3, 15 are crimson. 4 to 12, & 16 are copper.

Braid 16AB: 1, 4 are peach. 2, 3, 10, 11 are black. 5 to 9, & 12 to 16 are red.

Braid 16AB: 1, 2, 9, 10 are black. 3, 4, 11, 12 are grey. 5, 6, 13, 14 are light grey. 7, 8, 15, 16 are crimson.

Braid 16AC (variation): 1, 2, 5, 6 are peach. 3, 4, 7, 8, 11, 12, 15, 16 are black. 9, 10, 13, 14 are red.

Braid 16AC: 1, 2, 4, 11, 13, 14 are copper. 3, 5, 6, 9, 10, 12 are brown. 7, 8 are crimson. 15, 16 are black.

Braid 16AD: 1, 13 are grey. 2, 3, 4, 6, 7, 8, 10, 11, 12, 14, 15, 16 are crimson. 5, 9 are peach.

Braid 16 AD: 1, 5, 9, 13 are crimson. 2, 3, 15, 16 are black. 4, 8, 10, 14 are grey. 6, 7, 11, 12 are light grey.

Photograph 22. Orchids.
Braid 16N worked around a metal frame. The braid started as a hollow blunt end (see page 78) enabling the ends of the braid to be hidden inside the beginning.

Photograph 24. Beaded Ends.
MAIN PICTURE:
Braid 16V: 1 to 4, & 9 to 12 are cream. 5, 16 are mauve. 6, 7, 8, 13, 14, 15 are black.
INSERT:
Braid 16B: 1, 2, 5, 6, 9, 10, 13, 14 are mauve. 3, 4, 7, 11, 12, 15 are cream. 8, 16 are black.
Beaded ends are discussed on page 81.

Photograph 25. Covered Ball Ends.
Braid 8F: Bobbins 1, 5 are each one rope of metallic gold.
Bobbins 3, 7 are each 4 ropes of cream.
Bobbins 2, 4, 6, 8 are each 2 ropes of peach.
Details of covered ball ends can be found on page 84.

Photograph 26. Knotted Ends.
Braid 8K: 1, 2 are navy. 3, 5, 6, 8 are pink. 4, 7 are burgundy.
The knotted ends are braid 8H: 1, 5 are burgundy. 2, 3, 6, 7 are pink. 4, 8 are navy.
Details of knot found on page 84.

Photograph 27.
TOP: Direct attachment/Distorted braid. Example 1.
Braid 16G: 1 to 4, & 9 to 12 are red. 5 to 8, & 13 to 16 are black.
Details of distorted braid on page 91 & direct attachment on page 84.
CENTRE: Split Ends.
Braid 16G: 1, 4, 9, 12 are black. 2, 3, 10, 11 are white. 5 to 8, & 13 to 16 are red.
Details of split ends on page 81.
BOTTOM: Covered Ends.
Here a variation of braid 16F is worked using the following sequence of movements:
1, 2, 3, 4, 5, 6.
1, 2, 3, 4, 5, 6.
1, 2, 3, 4, 5, 6, 7, 8.
The initial colour layout is as follows: 1 to 4, & 9 to 12 are grey silk. 6, 7, 14, 15 are black silk. 5, 8, 13, 16 are red cord.
Details of covered ends on page 81.

Photograph 28. Zig-Zags.
Braid 8F worked with extra moves described on page 86.
The initial colour layout is as follows: 1, 2, 5, 6 are black. 3, 4, 7, 8 are white.

Photograph 37.
TOP LEFT.
Black Onyx Necklace.
Braid 8H: 1, 4, 5, 8 are black. 2, 3, 6, 7 are white.
Braid 8F: 1, 5 are black. 2, 3, 4, 6, 7, 8 are white.
Braids joined with reef knots and linked

with sterling silver fittings and black onyx bead.
TOP RIGHT: Combined Braid.
Example 4.
First braid of 8F: 1, 2, 5, 6 are blue. 3, 4, 7, 8 are purple.
The final combined braid (Example 4, page 97) is 16N, starting with a true blunt end (see page 78).
BOTTOM LEFT.
Holes. Example 1.
Braid 16D: 1 to 4, & 9 to 12 are dark blue. 5 to 8, & 13 to 16 are light blue.
Working details on page 93.
BOTTOM RIGHT.
Bracelets.
Beads. Example 3 (page 92).
Braid 8F: 1 loaded with black onyx beads. 2, 6 are pink. 3, 4, 7, 8 are green. 5 is mauve.
Braid 8F: 1 loaded with lapis lazuli beads. 2, 6 are black. 3, 7 & 8 are blue. 4 is mauve, 5 is green.

Photograph 38. Tufted Braids.
A combination of tufted and other braids couched onto a silk bag. The Tufted Earrings have the following initial colour layout:
1, 2, 4, 5 are dark blue. 3, 6, 9, 12 are light blue. 7, 8, 10, 11 are a mix of pink and mauve.
Working details on page 90.

Photograph 39. Chokers.
Made using a combination of braid 16C, 8F and 8H. Braid 16C had bobbins 1, 2, 9, 10 finer than the rest to exaggerate to spiral structure.

Bibliography
and further reading

ASHLEY, CLIFFORD: The Ashley Book of Knots. *Faber & Faber.*

CHEN, LYDIA: Chinese Knotting. *Echo Publications, Taiwan.*

KLIOT, JULES & KAETHE: Kumihimo, Techniques of Japanese Plaiting. *Self.*

MARTIN, CATHERINE: Kumihimo - Japanese Silk Braiding Techniques. *Old Hall Press, Hatfield. 1986.*

OWEN, RODRICK: The Big Book of Braids. *Cassell. 1994.*

SAHASHI, KEI: Exquisite - The World of Japanese Kumihimo Braiding. *Kodansha International Ltd. 1988.*

SAKAI, AIKO: Sohbi Braiding Books 1-5. *Nihon Vogue.*

SPEISER, NOEMI: The Manual of Braiding. *Self.*

TOKORO, HOKO: Kumihimo in Japan. *Ogaki Unesco Association Japan. 1993.*